Playing With Words

Also by the authors:

Paul Williams
Parallax, young adult speculative fiction series: Zharmae Publishing, Los Angeles, 2014, 2015
Cokcraco, literary fiction: Lacuna Publishing, Sydney, Australia, 2013
Soldier Blue, memoir: New Africa Books, Cape Town, 2007
The Secret of Old Mukiwa, Young Adult mystery: College Press, Harare, 2001

Shelley Davidow

Non Fiction

Whisperings in the Blood, biographical memoir: University of Queensland Press, Australia 2016
Raising Stress-Proof Kids, non-fiction parenting book: Exisle Books, NSW, Australia, 2014, Familius Books USA, 2015 (published in Vietnam and Poland 2015)
The Eye of the Moon, non-fiction immigrant memoir: Rainy Nights Press, Oregon, USA, 2007
My Life with AIDS—Charmayne Broadway's Story, non-fiction biography: Southern Book Publishers, South Africa, 1998

Adult Fiction

To Have and to Hold, romance – pacesetter: Macmillan, UK, 1998

Young Adult Fiction

Lights Over Emerald Creek, speculative YA fiction: Hague Publishing, Australia 2014
Spirit of the Mountain, young adult novel: Steiner Books, USA, 2007
In the Shadow of Inyangani, Macmillan Writer's Prize for Africa: Macmillan, UK, 2003
The Rainy Season, young adult novel – Trendsetter: Macmillan, UK, 1997
Spirit of the Mountain, young adult novel: Tafelberg, South Africa, 1998; Floris Books, UK, 2003
Remember the Light, young adult novel: Macmillan Boleswa, South Africa, 1992
Freefalling, young adult novel – runner-up 1991 Young Africa Award: Maskew Miller Longman, South Africa, 1991

Children's Fiction

The Wise Enchanter, children's fantasy novel: Bell Pond Books, USA, 2006
A Handful of Sweets, Today's Children series: Macmillan, UK, 2002
Let's Play One-Bounce, Today's Children series: Macmillan, UK, 2002
Two Readers for Uganda, Primary 2, Macmillan, UK 1st edition, 2001; 2nd edition 2002
Water for Monique, Caribbean 'Hop, Step, Jump' series, co-authored with Cathy Parrill: Macmillan, UK, 2002
Writing on Wood, Today's Children series: Macmillan, UK, 2002
6 graded readers for Uganda, Password series: Macmillan, UK, 1998
The Red Shadow, Today's Children series: Macmillan UK & UNHCR (United Nations High Commissioner for Refugees) English and French editions, 1998
Kiki and the Storm, Reader for 'Ready … Go' series: Macmillan, UK, 1998
The Cowrie Seekers, Reader for 'Hop, Step, Jump' series: Macmillan, UK, 1997
Search for the Stone Bird, Reader for 'Hop, Step, Jump' series: Macmillan UK, 1997
The River, Reader for 'Ready … Go' series: Macmillan, UK, 1997

Early Readers and Phonetic Chapter Books

The Secret Wish, children's phonetically based chapter book: Personhood Press, USA, 2014
6 phonetic readers: *Sam Cat and Nat Rat; Ned and Fred; Len Bug and Jen Slug; Jake the Snake; Snails in the Rain; Tim's Boat:* Personhood Press, USA, 2012
The Secret Pet, children's phonetically based chapter book: Personhood Press, USA, 2012
The Secret Door, children's phonetically based chapter book: Personhood Press, USA, 2012

Playing With Words
An Introduction to Creative Writing Craft

Paul Williams

Shelley Davidow

© Paul Williams & Shelley Davidow 2016

All rights reserved. No reproduction, copy or transmission of this publication may be made without written permission.

No portion of this publication may be reproduced, copied or transmitted save with written permission or in accordance with the provisions of the Copyright, Designs and Patents Act 1988, or under the terms of any licence permitting limited copying issued by the Copyright Licensing Agency, Saffron House, 6–10 Kirby Street, London EC1N 8TS.

Any person who does any unauthorized act in relation to this publication may be liable to criminal prosecution and civil claims for damages.

The authors have asserted their rights to be identified as the authors of this work in accordance with the Copyright, Designs and Patents Act 1988.

First published 2016 by
PALGRAVE

Palgrave in the UK is an imprint of Macmillan Publishers Limited, registered in England, company number 785998, of 4 Crinan Street, London, N1 9XW.

Palgrave Macmillan in the US is a division of St Martin's Press LLC, 175 Fifth Avenue, New York, NY 10010.

Palgrave is a global imprint of the above companies and is represented throughout the world.

Palgrave® and Macmillan® are registered trademarks in the United States, the United Kingdom, Europe and other countries.

ISBN 978–1–137–53253–4 hardback

ISBN 978–1–137–53252–7 paperback

This book is printed on paper suitable for recycling and made from fully managed and sustained forest sources. Logging, pulping and manufacturing processes are expected to conform to the environmental regulations of the country of origin.

A catalogue record for this book is available from the British Library.

A catalog record for this book is available from the Library of Congress.

Printed in China

Contents

1	**Playing with Words: Flaubert's *'le mot juste'***	1
	Word-association Wonders	4
	Collecting Words	5
	Words to Sentences	6
	Playing with Words	10
	No Ideas but in Things	13
	Le Mot Juste	14
	Word Order	16
	English Words: Past and Future	17
2	**Stunning Sentences and Powerful Paragraphs – and the role of the Grammar Police**	19
	Heavy Sentence Construction	23
	Rule: Don't Use Run-ons	26
	Short Sentences	28
	Spontaneous Prose	30
	Poetry	31
	The Souls of Sentences	32
	Powerful Paragraph Country	32
3	**Sound and Rhythm in Voice**	36
	Accents, Syllables and Stress	37
	Repetition and Refrains	40
	Rhythm: The Writer's Beat	41
	The Voice of the Villanelle	42
	Punctuating Prose and the Creation of Voice	44
4	**Angling for a View – Who's Telling?**	48
	It's My Story and I'm Telling It: First-person Perspective	50
	I'm Telling, but Don't Believe Everything I Say: The Unreliable First Person	51
	He Stepped onto the Train: An Objective Third-person Account	52
	She Wished He Would Stop Staring: Close Third-person Point of View	53
	You're Happy and You Know it: The Ubiquitous Second Person	55

Unique Angles in Space: Moving Narrators into Adjacent
　　　　Territories　57
　　　Being the All-knowing, All-seeing Omniscient Creator
　　　　(Who Is Everywhere at All Times)　57
　　　Narrators Who Aren't There and Epistolary Texts　58
　　　Let Me Tell You Something: The Intrusive Narrator　62
　　　A Myriad of Impressions: First-person Stream of
　　　　Consciousness　65
　　　Past or Present Tense　67

5　**Really Bad Writing: Melodrama, Sentimentality,
　　Overwriting and Lazy Writing**　**72**
　　　Melodramatically Sentimental Overwriting　73
　　　Staggeringly Bad Writing　76
　　　Writer's Elbow　77
　　　Indulgent Overwriting　78
　　　Lazy Writing　81
　　　Lazy Writing Protection　82
　　　Clichés　82
　　　Popular Writing　85
　　　Other Deadeners and Killjoys of Writing Pleasure　85
　　　Conclusion: There's a Troll in My Bathroom　87

6　**Silences and the Spaces Between**　**88**
　　　Minimalism, Icebergs and Truth　90
　　　Unleashing the Editor　93
　　　Minimalist Grammar and Some Breaking of Rules (Again)　94
　　　Litotes　96
　　　Dispassion　96
　　　The Art of Omission and Stitching round Black Holes　97
　　　From Black Holes to White Spaces　98
　　　Kill Your Darlings　99
　　　Less and Less is More and More　100
　　　About the Fine Art of Elimination　101
　　　Maximalism　102

7　**Painting the Picture: Images that Light up the
　　Sensory Cortex**　**104**
　　　From the Analogous to the Allegorical: Expanding the
　　　　Figurative　108
　　　Symbols, Dreams and the Power of the Single Image　110
　　　Becoming the Master (or Mistress) of Allusions　112

	Deconstructing Metonymy and Synecdoche	112
	Hysterical Hyperbole	113
	Clichés: The Classic Route to Ruining Good Writing	114
	The Sensations of Our Senses	114
	More Than Believable Backdrops: Establishing a Worthy Setting	115
	The Magic of Movies	116
	Exterior Landscape as Mirror of the Interior	119
8	**Those Who Speak: Avatars, Characters, Selves**	**121**
	Being Many Characters	122
	Revealing Character through Dialogue-Driven Narrative	123
	The Mechanics of Dialogue: Avoiding Some Classic Deadeners and When It's Time to *Be* the Punctuation Police	124
	Being a Dialogue Diva on Punctuation and Speech Tags	126
	Too Much Verisimilitude in Dialogue	126
	Contractions	127
	Misspellings	127
	Bad Grammar	127
	Giving Characters Life	127
	What He Thinks, What She Believes: The Inner Lives of Characters	129
	Taking Action	130
	Direct Exposition Description	131
	What's in a Name?	131
	Habits, Tics, Idiosyncrasies	132
	How Others See Them	134
	Character through Juxtaposition and Relationships	135
	The Evolution of Character: Changes over Time	136
9	**Building Narratives: Movement through Time and Place**	**138**
	Why We Need Conflict	140
	Intuitive Plotting	141
	Practice-led Research	141
	The Two Subjects	142
	Pyramid Schemes: Formulaic Plotting	144
	Hero with a Thousand Faces	144
	Sucking Readers into the Vortex	146
	Beginnings and Endings	147
	Famous Last Words	148
	Moving through Time and Space	150
	Creating Suspense	150

In Medias Res	151
Flashback	152
Foreshadowing	152
Cliffhangers	154
Themes and Hidden Narrative Movements	155
Creating Theme	155
Romance, Thrillers, True Crime and Other Genre Fiction	156

10 Innovations   **158**
- The Postmodern Mind — 159
- Palimpsest — 160
- Bowerbirding, Bricolage and Plagiarism — 161
- Polyphonic Voice — 162
- The Composite Novel — 166
- Borrowings: Ergodic Texts — 167
- Antinomacy: Reverse Chronology — 168
- Ecriture Feminine: Writing the Body — 169
- Magic Realism — 171
- Creative Nonfiction — 172
- Historiographic Metafiction — 174
- Conclusion: Pushing the Boundaries — 175

Appendix — 178

References — 183

Index — 189

1
Playing with Words: Flaubert's 'le mot juste'

> **Freewrite #1: Write without stopping for two minutes. Begin with this prompt:**
> *I've never confessed this, and this is something you don't know about me, but...*

To introduce ourselves:

SHELLEY

I left South Africa, where I was born, a few months after I had won a national literary award for my first book. The most compelling reason for leaving: a journalist friend of ours, who was black, was shot dead in front of his home by white Apartheid government agents. He had been writing about the value of a creative, freethinking education for all South Africans so that the whole nation might achieve freedom and self-fulfilment. This was too much for those in power who wanted to keep black people oppressed and servile. So they silenced him. I couldn't live in a place where writers were killed for their words. So I left my country as soon as I could, having learned at the very beginning of my writing career what power lay in the written word.

PAUL

I grew up in a civil war, and when I was eighteen, I was conscripted by a minority government to fight against the majority population. During the two years I spent in that war, I kept a journal in which I recorded everything I saw, and heard and felt. Fellow soldiers mocked me for doing it ('He's writing his memoirs!'), and when I left at the end, I had to sign a declaration that I would never write about the things I had seen. But I felt I had to record, to witness in words; otherwise, I would not remember or even believe what I had experienced. Memory plays tricks on you. I am so glad I did write things down, because that journal became a memoir (Soldier Blue). *Scenes in the book that seem far-fetched are documented exactly, word for word, down to the last details of what played on the radio when the bullets hit; what the smell of the dawn was like; how the bullets sounded, whistling through the grass above my shelter; or the heavy weight of someone dying in my arms.*

I wanted to describe the experience of the real world in words – the wonder or the pain of being alive – and capture it like a photo, freezing a moment in time. I also wrote to try to understand things, to work out problems, to heal wounds in my soul. I wrote every day, first as a journalist, then as a creative writer, a historian, a self-therapist, a magician conjuring and an explorer, finding new territories of the mind. Words have always fascinated me.

There are many roads to becoming a skilled and proficient writer. Some writers are born out of their voracious reading and intuitively develop a style, a voice, a way with words that comes from years of immersion in other writers' voices. The question is, can good writing be taught? And the answer is 'yes, of course.' Ursula Le Guin writes in her exhilarating creative writing book *Steering the Craft*: 'A skill is something you know how to do. Skill in writing frees you to write what you want to write. It may also show you what you want to write. Craft enables art' (Le Guin, 1998). Any person who learns a craft can put it to good use. We can learn by doing or from a good teacher or from both. This book offers tools that can be kept by a bedside and used at any time.

Chapter 1 is all about acquiring the skills to make our words do what we want them to do, regardless of genre, format or style. To really harness the power of words, we need to become skilled craftspeople who can mould and shape our material so that the finished product is as close to what we imagined as possible.

As writers, we make realities with words. We can change thoughts, lives – even the direction of a whole country – simply by placing our words in a certain order. This is a mind-bending thought. So we're going to zoom in on words: by themselves, and in context. Because the miraculous concept is this: although words are the essential tools to construct intangible things like thoughts and ideas and imagined alternative realities, they are ultimately just the keys we use to unlock limitless realms of stories and ideas. And so, our job, ironically, is to work with words so expertly that they eventually vanish. Everyone knows that when we read something incredible, the printed words in front of us disappear.

The writers who learn this first are poets – because in a poem every word counts. Poets know how a well-placed verb can make our real, noisy, tangible world of bedrooms, chairs, cars and offices dissolve into oblivion. The intense focus on words in poetry can make better writers out of all of us.

Whether we are writing fiction, memoir, non-fiction or genre fiction, poetry provides the tools for writers of all kinds to sharpen skills and zoom in on the power of words. It's in the detail of a single word choice that a writer can transform something dull into something sharp, regardless of form and genre. Using poetic techniques, we can improve our wordsmithery – and when we hit it right, words vanish in the wake of stories, images and ideas.

A word on its own is like a single star in deep space; if there's no one to see it, does it even exist? Of course there's power in that word, but without context, without us bringing our own intricate lives and thoughts to that word, its power remains dormant. Once we create context, bring our experience of living in the world to a word, each word has the power to transform into what we want it to be.

Mark Twain once said, 'The difference between the right word and almost the right word is the difference between lightning and a lightning bug [firefly]' (Bainton, 2007: 87–8). In our writing, we want the exact word, *le mot juste*.

For fun, let's take a random word – *jade* – and play with it. Its denotative (direct, factual) meaning is obvious: it's a green, semi-precious stone.

But *jade* has almost limitless connotative meanings that depend on readers and writers for its revelations. It may have emotional associations for one person that will be different for someone else. *Jade* may evoke images of green, of opulence, or jealousy, or the memory of love for someone with that name.

If we place another word next to *jade*, suddenly context emerges, as does rhythm, and then meaning: *cruel jade*. Now these two words could lead to a sentence: *The cruel jade knife cut into her hand*. *Jade* could also be a person's name, so by making the *J* a capital, the meaning of the two words together would change *jade* entirely: *cruel Jade*. This sentence might come to mind: *Cruel Jade – she left him again*.

If we use *jade* as an adjective or an adverb, it means something else:

Jaded cruelty.
His love was jaded.

Putting two unlikely words together can create an innovative association and lead to spontaneous creations, which may never otherwise have seen the light. The exercise that follows liberates words from the conventional comfortable positions they might usually occupy in our minds.

> ### GUTTER FLAVOUR: ASSOCIATIVE WORD EXERCISE
>
> Below is a list of arbitrary nouns and adjectives. Place any two together, and keep doing that to see what emerges. The image of, say, a gutter cowboy may be the inspiration for a new novel!
>
> | | |
> |---|---|
> | city | dirt |
> | cowboy | clean |
> | kind | guitar |
> | flavour | gutter |
> | meander | concrete |

Whether we're writing an advertisement, a political speech, a novel or a poem, we select certain words based on a myriad of factors. We choose words not for their denotative meaning alone, but for their associative emotional connotations.

Word-association Wonders

Most of us have had the experience of knowing we don't have the right word, and the one we want is on the *tip of our tongue* (an interesting expression in itself). In trawling for the word (which may just come to us in the middle of the night or when we are doing something unrelated), most often we have to trace back through our previous intricate thought processes to find it. We're often disturbed until we actively seek out that word and fit it, like a piece of rock into a hole in the wall. More often we retrieve this word by association with another.

PAUL

I used to play a game with friends called word association. Each person would say a word, and the next person would spontaneously say whatever word came to mind by connotation – connecting words by rhythm, sound, meaning or arbitrary emotional association:

For example: jade, spade, sam, girl, boy, servant, racism, mean, greens, bitter, sweet, revenge, hate, love, dove, shove, shovel, spade, detective, no shit Sherlock, dream on sunshine, teletubbies.

> **COWBOY and THUG EXERCISES**
>
> Start with the word *cowboy* or *feminist* or *thug* or *jade* or *girl* or *organic*. Write down, as fast as you can, words that follow from this – whatever words, images, associations come to mind when you think of this word. This allows the associative, connotative meanings that exist uniquely in each of our minds to rise to the surface. Now look up the denotative meaning of the word in a dictionary.

Collecting Words

Many writers collect words like magpies collect shiny objects for their nests. Here are three random words that could be rediscovered depending on how they are used:

Flutter and *flitter* and *fleeting*

Eyelids flutter, hearts flutter, but so can buildings in earth tremors, and so can colours. People can flitter from one conversation to another at parties, and love can be fleeting; so can glances or even civilizations.

> *Flutter* – from the medieval English 'to throw someone into confusion ... to float (on waves); irregular heart beat'.
> *Flitter* – 'to fly'.
> *Fleeting* – 'transient'.

Another example of two words that could be interesting and that many people confuse are *tortuous* and *torturous*.

What is the difference between them? They're not interchangeable! One is 'meandering' and the other 'painful'. Although, one might add, a path, or an argument, or a book can be both tortuous and torturous, but there is a difference.

LIST OF BEST WORDS EXERCISE

Write down a list of your favourite words, past and present. Once you have the list, use the words to create a paragraph. Sometimes just playing with words gives rise to the most creative ideas.

Write down two words with similar meanings that are often confused. Write sentences using both words.

Love words. Collect them. They are the building blocks of all writing.

Words to Sentences

As words evolve into sentences, rhythm emerges. And as we begin and end those sentences, we evolve meaning. The sentence below could have been a note, a string of words left on anyone's kitchen counter:

> *Just a note: I have gone for a walk up the hill; I didn't want to miss the sunset. I wish you had come with me – it was magnificent: magenta and white magic.*

But if we rewrite it as a poem, breaking lines leads us to a focus on certain words, which then gives them weight and significance:

I have gone
For a walk
Up the hill

I didn't want
To miss the sunset

I wish you had come
With me
It was magnificent
Magenta and white
Magic

The only change from simple sentence to poem is in the form – the way the words are arranged, the spaces between and the way the writer has broken the lines into stanzas. But the whole rhythm alters so that each word takes on weight; each word is now given some significance or meaning that the prose does not have.

It's a poem inspired by the poet William Carlos Williams (Note: check out 'This is Just to Say'). It seems as though it should make no difference where we break our lines, as long as the sentences are clear, but placing words in certain places gives them significance and rhythm and a visual, concrete quality.

PLACEMENT OF WORDS EXERCISE

- Write for fifteen seconds without stopping, and create a sentence or two about anything that is in your head.

- When you've finished, cut the sentences into shorter lines. Create stanzas. Decide how many words you want on each line and how many spaces you want between words, lines and stanzas. Break the flow. Put one word on a line, or ten.

- Read the poem aloud.

PAUL

Let me confess: I always wanted to be a novelist. I hated poetry, felt it was a waste, irrelevant, useless. Who reads poetry anymore? So to my detriment, I read only prose fiction. But my writing suffered. Poetry is the heart of prose. Its rhythms, spaces, sentence breathing, rhyme, word play was all lost to me as I sought to write down stories, ideas, plots, paying very little attention to words themselves. They were just a means to communicate. How wrong I was.

I had to learn to love words. And I did. By writing poetry.

SHELLEY

When we lived in the United States, I was invited into a poetry group in Oregon, which was made up of fiction writers. (We were the 'Poultry Group', a bunch of 'chicks' representing five decades). We came together because one of the writers had writer's block, and several of us were in the writer's doldrums. The thought was that poetry would ensure we each would write one small thing a month. Each month we chose a different poetic form and had to

8 *Playing With Words*

learn how to use minimal language for maximum effect. After three years, the writer with writer's block had a New York Times *bestseller, and the rest of us had had novels or poetry accepted or published. My most helpful tools for writing fiction and non-fiction were gained in the Poultry Group.*

Focusing on the power of each word for the purpose of poetry made me a sharper, more exact fiction and non-fiction writer.

One way of highlighting the visual aspect of words is to take a look at concrete poetry. This is a form of poetry in which the way the words are arranged on the page creates meaning just as much as the words themselves. The reader has a kinaesthetic experience because the visual *is* the subject matter. For some exciting examples of concrete poems, resources are at the end of this chapter.

```
PA per flut
Ttering, he   re and th   ere
Breeze blo   w ing every w   here
Gu  st o ver  clu   terred wri ter' s
table
Wo   rds sca    ttered thoughts
Sh at t e red
```

```
                    Jaded love
   My heart s t – r –  r-  e – t – t – c – h – h  e     s
                i                                r
             n                             a
               k           o
                 s
```

crashes
every time you walk by
like   neck
   the   your
      cruel   around
           jade   wear
                    you

> **CONCRETE POETRY EXERCISE**
>
> Create a poem where the words on the page represent, in image form, the subject matter you have chosen. Any subject matter can be used: you could write a poem about a tree, a flower, a gust of wind, a rainbow, a cat or a suitcase.

If we choose our words carefully and place them in sentences in positions where they will be potent – if we are aware of the space they occupy, and the power of their connotations and the emotional weight they carry, we become magicians of a sort, capable of transporting both ourselves and our readers into alternate imaginative realities.

PAUL

In my first novel, I began with a concrete poem. I wanted to portray the dislocation of someone in a war who has been shot in the head, loses and regains consciousness, and is rescued by helicopter. Here is how I did it:

THUD
    THUD
        THUD

Over here Doc doc.

Here comes the chopper to chop off your head

                                    No, over here

No
Use
He's
a
goner
        breathe dammit breathe
                                    THUD
                                THUD
                        THUD

I wanted the reader's eyes/attention/consciousness to be similarly dislocated.

Later, after many edits and rewrites, and advice from prudent editors, I rewrote the whole passage in conventional prose. The editors told me the concrete poem was rather gimmicky and crude, like using CAPS in texting or like using many exclamations marks to draw attention (!!!!!), and that the dislocation could be portrayed in conventional prose just as effectively, using word choice and strategic word placement. So the final concrete poem ended up as the following:

> Thud, thud, thud.
> Over here, Doc. Doc!
> Here comes the chopper to chop off your head.
> No, over here.
> His soul flew up and perched above the scene on a crooked Msasa tree branch, and smiled down at the vain attempts to resuscitate his lifeless body.
> 'No use, he's a goner.'
> 'Breathe, dammit, breathe.'
> Thud, thud, thud.

But it was useful in helping me see words as playthings, like pieces of a jigsaw, place markers I could rearrange on the page to see what effect they created. In other words, I, who cared little for 'poetry', was writing poetry.

So if you're a poet or you want to write poetry, you're ahead of this game. If you want to write fiction, do what Charles Baudelaire, the French writer suggests: 'Always be a poet, even in prose' (Moore, 2009: 190).

Poetry is the essence of the writer's craft, the quiet breathing we need to train ourselves to do. It's the best use of language and the distilled essence of craft.

Playing with Words

Words aren't always serious business. Often we wrestle to find the right word, agonize over sentence structure, fight to make the words conform to our intentional meaning. But sometimes the best way to make words work for us is to play with them. Words respond well to being placed unconventionally or even changed altogether. Their power often lies in their ability to mean one thing if looked at one way, or another thing if looked at another way. Sometimes we need to use them for the sheer joy of their sound. And if a word we are looking for doesn't exist, we can make one up. Shakespeare did. Though the jury is still out as to whether he was truly the inventor of the thousands of words ascribed to him or just the first person to write them down, it doesn't matter much. He is still the official source famous for contributing over 2000 words to the Oxford English Dictionary. Where would we be without *advertising, zany* or *undress*? There may have been many more, but words like *infamonize* ('to make infamous') and *congreeted* ('to exchange hellos and make small talk') never caught on. Language is all the richer for the contributions of those who have the courage to create.

New words are known as neologisms, and the art of making up new words is called neolexia; it follows then, that the maker of new words is called a neologist. Lewis Carroll, the author of *Alice's Adventures in Wonderland*, like Shakespeare, was one of them.

> 'When I use a word,' Humpty Dumpty said in rather a scornful tone, 'it means just what I choose it to mean – neither more nor less.'
> 'The question is,' said Alice, 'whether you *can* make words mean so many different things.'
> 'The question is,' said Humpty Dumpty, 'which is to be master – that's all.' (Carroll, 1993)

Lewis Carroll's 'Jabberwocky' is a neologistic poem consisting of mostly made-up and nonsense words, which have a powerful, comedic and associative quality.

Without knowing their meaning, we can intuit an associative sense of what the word stands for from both sound and context. *Slithy Toves* which *gyre and gimble* in weather that is *brillig* are self-explanatory, even though no such words exist in the English language (Carroll, 1993).

> **BEING LEWIS CARROLL AND WILLIAM SHAKESPEARE WORD INVENTION EXERCISE**
>
> Write a 10- to 14-line rhyming nonsense poem, making up words, and/or combining words you like, for example *wonderlicious, scrambunctious, chuffish*. Add words, which are onomatapoieac, like *splash, slap, whistle* (this may well be how all words originated, so have no fear: be the creator). Feel free to evolve new nonsense words out of old ones. (If slithy toves like to gimble, are they then *gimblers*?)

Children are often in love with the sound of words, and also the way they tumble out after each other, the way tongue twisters tickle or rhymes ricochet ... and all of us were children once, so it shouldn't be too hard to remember hearing a new word and loving it for its own sake.

The delight of nursery rhymes, words used in tongue-twisted and rhyming ways, and limericks does not belong exclusively to the territory of small children: we're allowed to play too. We can immerse ourselves in words for words' sake, love them, twist them and turn them. So, in honour of that love, and with reference to the eternally ticklish Dr. Seuss's *Fox in Socks* and *Green Eggs and Ham*, and the inventor of the limerick, Mr Edward Lear, here is an opportunity to delight in what you would have enjoyed as a child, with permission to be as obtuse, absurd or as zany as you like. The big idea behind this exercise is to tap into universal, primeval territory where we can experience the creative power of word making at work.

SHELLEY

Confession: I wrote this limerick when I was in my late teens. I was attempting to write a book called 101 Rude and Not-So-Rude Limericks, *but after completing about 60, I had used up every creative and zany thought I'd ever had, and there seemed to be not a single limerick left in me. Here's a remnant of that abandoned volume. Rereading the limerick reminds me of the inherent and childish delight I took in a form which allows for and encourages delicious and slightly revolting images.*

> There once was a woman called Dot
> Who was an incredible clot,
> She swallowed a slug
> On the side of her mug
> And it stuck in her throat like snot.

PERMISSION TO WRITE A RIDICULOUS LIMERICK EXERCISE

Use the appropriate rhyme (aa/bb/a) and the more-or-less appropriate rhythm:

Lines 1 and 2: eight syllables

> Lines 3 and 4: five syllables
> Line 5: eight syllables
>
> Even if the meaning is nonsense, have fun. Play with the words for their own sake. Get the feel of how they delight. Be silly. Enjoy them.
>
> *or*
>
> Take a word and play with it. Turn it inside out; say it aloud; distort it; make associations and connotations with it; place it in a sentence in an unusual place.

No Ideas but in Things

Sometimes our writing 'doesn't work,' or readers cannot 'get into it' or feel its power. This may be because the words are not genuinely suited to our purpose; perhaps the bulk of the writing includes words that are too generic. We can easily rely on abstract words like *love* or *hate*, or *good* or *bad*, or use tired words like *nice* and *happy*, which have mostly lost their connotative and denotative power through overuse. Then our writing can quickly become dull. An inspiring idea that originates with the Imagists, a group of poets in the early twentieth century, is that there are 'no ideas but in things' (Williams, 2000). Meaning resides in words, not in our ideas.

With this in mind, words become immediate, sensual, sensory, physical, concrete things that depict the immediate, sensual, concrete world as it is. When we use words in this way, we don't stray into abstract concepts.

> Jade: an apparition at my doorstep drenched in night rain – her hair knotted and shimmering in the refracted light from the window upstairs.

Through these words we get a picture, not an intellectual concept, but an image; we can see Jade's knotted hair. The word *apparition* is also deliberate. It means a ghost or ghostlike image of a person. But it also has a religious connotation – a magical opening of the supernatural realm – or a revelation.

> **WRITING IMAGES EXERCISE**
>
> Write a few lines about a person, object or setting, using an image to describe it. The line could be something simple, like this: *The lamp sits on my desk, dishevelled.*
>
> Find the words that fit, that resonate.

Le Mot Juste

In the writer's eternal quest to find the right word at the right place and time, we can learn from a group of writers who strove to find the right word to capture a moment of 'reality'.

Just as the Imagists restored poetry to its immediate, sensory words, the French literary realists in the mid-nineteenth century (writers such as Gustave Flaubert, Guy de Maupassant, Emile Zola) brought new life to fiction, and in particular to the new form of the short story. Gustave Courbet insists that writing needs to be 'an essentially *concrete* art [that] can only consist of the representation of real and existing things' (1861).

Here, for example, is Flaubert's advice to Maupassant:

> When you pass a grocer sitting in front of his door, a concierge smoking his pipe, or a cab rank, show me that grocer, that concierge, their attitude, their physical appearance and by the skill of the picture you draw of them, their whole moral nature as well and do this in such a way that I cannot confuse them with any other grocer or concierge; and *with a single word* show me how one cab horse is different from the fifty others ahead or behind it. (De Maupassant, 2008) [emphasis added]

How can we show a particular person or thing is unique with a single word?

Here is an example of how someone might write who isn't paying too much attention to the power of each word: 'I rang up her purchase at the till and gave her the jar and her change.'

Okay, it's not bad, but the words are very ordinary, and someone has just strung them together. You get the idea, but that's all.

By contrast, here's how that idea could evolve:

> She perched behind the counter and whizzed the items across the scanner. This was a race: a challenge. Who could win? Me packing

them away or she scanning and beeping, hesitating that fraction of a second to hear the satisfying thunk as the smart computer recognized the item's barcode and grunted its approval. Yes. Yes. Her hands deft and skilled at turning over the package to expose the barcode, or if it was loose fruit, weighing it, tapping the code faster than I thought possible before I had time to throw the previous item in the bag. She looked up; I looked up. Her name badge was yellow: 'Hi I'm Minnie, how can I exceed your expectations today?' it read. She smiled as she saw me reading it. She wore it at a jaunty angle, as if to say this is a farce, I'm playing a game, and I can do it with panache.

Flaubert called this practice the quest for *'le mot juste'* (the right word). Here is a particular checkout person who cannot be mistaken for any other.

FRENCH CAFÉ EXERCISE

Sit at a café, and describe a person sitting opposite you, or describe a table or a coffee cup. Write about that particular cup or person, in detail, for a page. What do you see? Feel? Hear? Stretch your thinking and words. You may find yourself grappling for the right word. You may feel your word reservoir is inadequate. You may nail that description the first time. But try to be a Realist, a photographer who can capture the exact moment, colour, shape, depth, movement of that person or thing in words. Like a painter or sculptor, use words as clay or paint.

Flaubert also claimed that when the right word is found, though it will become invisible, as a reader is transported into a scene, a dialogue, that reader, seeing the images beyond the individual word, will feel its power.

Flaubert struggled with every word he wrote. Good writing, he said, is smooth on the surface, but underneath, a tiger lurks [*'lisse comme un marbre et furieux comme un tigre'* (Byatt, 2002).].

His technique is to make words work so well that the writing looks easy, and we slide into that other reality conjured up by the words. If we are at all aware of our clever or clumsy words or descriptions, then we have not written well.

Good writing may look effortless. When the words disappear into the picture for our readers, it's because we have pummelled and tussled with our writing, even wept over our ineptitude, to make it work.

On the surface, a finished piece may ultimately seem to flow like water somersaulting effortlessly over the edge of a flooded gutter, but underneath lurk thought tigers wrestled into position by our struggles.

> **FINDING THE RIGHT WORDS EXERCISE**
>
> Start with a simple sentence: 'She walked into the room. She placed her briefcase down on the table and went to get a drink.' Use a thesaurus and rewrite the scene, expanding it to about 300 words. The action of this scene is still the same, but the words you choose will ramp up the atmosphere and charge it so that it's visceral and evocative. Play. Replace commonplace, well-worn words, including verbs, with unusual ones. Find the 'right word'.

Word Order

Word order is everything. Position the word *only* in different places in a sentence, and it will change the meaning of that sentence completely:

> Only *Joe and I can eat tacos while watching TV.*
> *Joe and I can eat* only *tacos while watching TV.*
> *Joe and I can eat tacos* only *while watching TV.*

Words are slippery. We can slide them sideways into our narratives and place them in startling and unexpected relationships to each other. We can use them in any chosen order as long as the basic structure of a sentence exists to generate new meaning, to create layers of meaning, or irony or humour.

Below is a piece inspired by anti-apartheid activist Chris Van Wyk's protest poem 'In Detention' (Van Wyk, 1995). The form is a play on word order and repetition and works to rearticulate, to dislocate and mirror turbulence, to create irony and bend reality by reorganizing simple lines. 'He Lost Himself' is a tribute to a great poet.

> He stumbled into a glass door
> He lost himself
> He tripped over his broken heart while drinking
> He lost himself
> He tripped over his broken heart while drinking

He stumbled into a glass door
He lost himself while drinking
He tripped into a glass door
He lost himself in a glass door
He tripped into a glass door while drinking
He stumbled over his broken heart while tripping
He lost himself in a glass door
He drank into a glass door while tripping
He lost his broken heart while stumbling

> **STUMBLING INTO A GLASS DOOR EXERCISE**
>
> Write a poem like this, beginning with a short, ordinary phrase. Follow the form above so that the phrase is deconstructed and turned inside out. Feel free to make changes to the form if necessary.

Our job as writers is to bring words to life again and again; to wrestle with language until it works for us.

We can get ideas by actually playing with the words, by sitting down and just writing. The act of placing one word in front of another, the process of selecting each word by its weight, texture, meaning, feeling is a visceral, sensual and pleasurable process that aids writing well. The words come first. Language creates reality. Has a phrase ever stuck in your head and you think, 'I must use that phrase or begin a novel that way', without ever having an idea what the novel is about?

If we ever get stuck (writer's block), we can go back to word level, play with a sentence or a word, get it right and immerse ourselves in the process. The piece starts flowing again.

English Words: Past and Future

English is a wonderful medium to work in, because the language has such variety. It owes its existence to an amalgamation of Latin, French, Arabic and many other languages, which were spliced onto its Celtic and Anglo-Saxon/Germanic roots; every culture using English has coloured the language with its own words, and those words have often travelled back and forth between continents. Our history and culture is inscribed into our sentences, long histories that include Arabic, Indian, African and Asian influences live in the words we speak and write each day. Even when we don't know the history of a word, we can feel its weight. Look, for example, at the word *beef*. Meat eaters don't eat *cow*, they eat *beef*, from the French *boeuf*. The word emerged in English after the Norman Conquest in 1066, when French was the language of the nobility. Lots of now-English words relating to food – or should that be *cuisine*? – came from French. And then, as those words began to live in our language, we used them for other things. Beef, for example, is not just a cow that we eat. We can *beef up* something, and something can look *beefy* and have nothing to do with cows!

Words themselves have stories in them, and when we choose them, we're choosing those stories, most often without knowing it, but feeling it. Every day, English is remade, reborn at some level, as more and more words are added from various fields, sometimes at a phenomenal rate, and in countries where English is evolving into something new, which we may not even recognize. New words added to the OED (Oxford English Dictionary) in the last decade include *google* (as a verb), *bromance, gaydar* and *unfriend* [on Facebook] (as a verb).

Our words are living, changing, evolving things. The big idea is that the way we use words locates us, and our writing, in a specific context, in a particular time and place. As writers, if we're sensitive to this change, to the power behind our words in the time we're alive, we can use them to shape the worlds we imagine, but also the ones we inhabit on a daily basis.

Here are some prose and poetry examples from great writers that have inspired us over time.

> See William Carlos Williams's 'This is Just to Say' and other imagist poems.
>
> For excellent examples of classic concrete poetry, look at e.e. cummings's 'r-p-o-p-h-e-s-s-a-g-r' or 'Mouse'.
>
> Lewis Carroll plays wonderful word games in *Alice's Adventures in Wonderland*. Read, in particular, his concrete poem 'The Mouse's Tail'.
>
> For connotative word-association examples, read Jamaica Kincaid's short story 'Girl.'
>
> For the quintessential word order poem see South African poet Chris Van Wyk's 'In Detention'.

2
Stunning Sentences and Powerful Paragraphs – and the role of the Grammar Police

> **Freewrite #2:**
>
> *The minute the phone rang, she knew her life would change forever …*

'I like sentences that don't budge though armies cross them,' says Virginia Woolf (2007: 99). Just as words are the building blocks of sentences, sentences become, in any work of fiction, non-fiction or poetry, the proxy of our thoughts – the distilled representatives of our ideas. A sentence that maintains its integrity over time is a worthy one! If we read back over pieces we've written long ago, and those pieces don't make us cringe or feel self-conscious, then we can be sure we've written sentences that won't budge even when armies (or time, or editors or readers for that matter) cross them!

The pace and tempo of a chapter or a whole book is impacted by the length of its sentences. We'll take a look at how sentence length can be used as a specific tool to create tension or give the reader a languorous look into the inner world of a character's thoughts. We'll also explore some common sentence structure errors and shed some light on the idea of 'right' and 'wrong' in grammar.

SHELLEY

I've been inspired by reading Steven Pinker (psycholinguist, scientist and author at Harvard University), who shows us that our instinct for language and grammar is innate … that by the time we're three years old, the whole structure of how to put sentences together is already native, and that the rules of grammar, or how we believe we should speak and write, are not made by some Uber-Grammar-God, but are the amalgamated opinions of dictionary writers, teachers and style-manual writers (Pinker, 1994). No one goes to jail for deliberately writing a whole paragraph made up of sentence fragments. So ... although grammar rules are there to guide us to clear expression, there are many rules that we writers can and do break. For example: Never start a sentence with 'But.' But I've written novels full of paragraphs that begin with 'But!' But more on all that later in the chapter!

When we are first taught how to write sentences, instructions are usually quite clear: subject-verb-object. Put a comma where you need to take a breath, and a full stop when you have said what you have to say. Simple. We are also taught the three cardinal sentence sins: the comma splice, run-on and fragment ... more on those to come.

A lot of what we know, of course, is native. We learn it intuitively and can write 'naturally'. For example, in which order do these adjectives go in a sentence?

He was a British, elderly, well-built, brown, tall, exceptional man.

We instinctively put them in an order that 'feels' correct, but believe it or not, there is a formula for putting them into the correct order:

General opinion
Specific opinion
Size
Shape
Age
Colour
Nationality
Material

He was an exceptional, well-built, tall, elderly, brown, British man.

However, there are a few rules we always seem to get wrong, and breaking these rules in ignorance is what makes our writing shoddy or amateurish and easily rejected by Grammar Police editors and publishers. But sentences are also meant to have rhythm, are meant to be spoken, and not just be grammatically correct. Every sentence therefore should contain some emotional density; it's easy to write grammatically correct, flat, boring sentences. How we make them emotionally rich is the subject of this chapter.

Let's take a close look at the grammar of 'correct' sentences, without fearing that we are being spied on by the Grammar Police. At some point all of us as writers take liberties with several rules, but that happens when we know exactly what we're doing for a desired effect. There is, after all, nothing more off-putting for an editor or publisher than to receive a submission from a would-be author that is full of sentence errors.

So, here's a question to get started: are these sentences?

> I am.
> It is.
> Both are.

All three are, actually. They all contain the necessary ingredients for a complete sentence: they each have a subject and a verb.

Sentence fragments are incomplete sentences that lack either the verb or subject. More commonly, a sentence fragment is a dependent clause belonging to a missing main sentence, such as:

> The road shimmering.
> While I was swimming.

Fragments are (annoyingly) common in writing by writers of all ages, and it's interesting to note that when fragments are unintentional, the writing looks amateurish and unprofessional, and yet in the hands of a highly skilled professional, fragments can be used to great effect. Example: *He arrived home drunk. Again.*

Comma splices are trickier: we cannot splice or join two independent clauses with a comma. Why? Because it's comma abuse.

Example: *He was on his way, she was not.*

This should read:

> *He was on his way; she was not.* (Use a semicolon to balance two independent clauses.)
>
> *He was on his way: she was not.* (Use a colon to suggest that the second clause follows from the first.)
>
> *He was on his way. She was not.* (This emphasizes the contrast in an abrupt way.)
>
> *He was on his way, but she was not.* (Use a conjunction to smooth the sentence.)
>
> *He was on his way … she was not.* (Pause to show the effect of her tardiness.)

These choices may seem trivial, but to the seasoned writer's eye, they are significant in every way. They help to create rhythm, tension, tone.

The only time a comma splice works is if it happens in a series of clauses, a list:

He was on his way, I was late, she was not.

A run-on sentence may not be what you think it is: it's not a long sentence that goes on and on, but one that neglects punctuation altogether. Here is an example of a run-on sentence that is very common and to be avoided:

He was on his way she was not.

Here is a passage where the writer disregards grammar rules to his detriment. It's obvious he is not in control.

> He walked along a road. Which was very narrow. 'Don't follow me.' He said. But the boy was following him, he could hear him panting behind him please, he whispered, don't come with me. Slinking along behind him.

And here is a passage where sentence fragments are used purposefully:

> He did escape. But only just. By the skin of his teeth. He slipped through the barrier as it crashed shut. Bang. But then they appeared, guns out, in hot pursuit. Run for it. Go, go go. His heart beating. His legs trembling. They were catching up. Twenty yards. Ten yards. Five.

Some writers use fragments to great effect. Read any page in Cormac McCarthy's *The Road*, and see how he uses fragments to create a disjointed post apocalyptic world where nothing flows.

So, good writers are not only aware of the rules but know how to break them when necessary. The trick is to do this intentionally, to be in control of the grammar and sentence structure.

FRAGMENTS EXERCISE

1. Write a paragraph (50–100 words) alternating between complete sentences and sentence fragments.

2. Rewrite the paragraph and make full sentences out of the fragments.

Decide which of the two pieces has the desired effect for that subject, and explain why.

The rhythm of a sentence is as important as its meaning, or content. In prose we can easily make the mistake of thinking that sentences are just ways to get ideas across.

In order to help us move beyond writing the same kind of sentences we have perhaps always written, the focus is on strengthening our capacity to build conscious, strong sentences and exercise our writing muscles in this area.

Heavy Sentence Construction

Modern writing tends to contain short, sharp, direct sentences. The quicker and clearer we get the meaning across, the better. We hardly use complex sentences anymore, and this may be because they are so hard to get right or because the attention span of readers is radically shorter than it used to be, trained and honed by rapidly changing visuals in films and brief tweets of big ideas in online media, so that by the time most modern readers get to the end of a very complex sentence, they may have lost the general idea entirely! Whew.

But sometimes complex sentences are necessary. They are vital to make our prose breathe.

For example, here's a long sentence that allows the reader to fall into the mind of the writer:

> If you fall in love with Jade, then you're in trouble: if it's only a passing crush, and you get out of there before she does too much damage to your heart, then you will get off with minor injuries, like a damaged ego and a few gashes that will heal – but what the hell are you going to do with that tattoo on your arm of an intertwined Frank and Jade brooch, huh?; if you fall heavily in love with her, then you're in big, big trouble, and you will have to live the rest of your life with a Jade-sized hole in your heart, a limp in your stride that will slow you down, and a stone in your gut that will sink you. The person who said time heals all wounds didn't know that Jade can stop all the clocks in your heart.

The form of this sentence is logical: it's a triangle, a perfect balance between a claim, and two conditional (if) clauses, and side comments, all built with commas, semicolons, dashes, parentheses and ellipses.

If ... , then ... :
If ... , then ... – ...   ;   if ... , then ...   .

The punctuation helps us build complex sentences without tripping up or using run-ons or comma splices or fragments. The semicolon does the balancing act in the middle, and the commas separate the 'if ... then' sections. It's interesting how the tagged-on comments are created through two devices that make the sentence pause for effect: the dash and the ellipses. The difference between these two sentence stoppers is that dashes can be used for an aside, or at the end of a sentence, whereas ellipsis dots (always three of them, and at the end of a sentence, four) are used to add an afterthought.

> **FALLING FOR JADE EXERCISE**
>
> Write an exact structural copy of the *Jade* paragraph, using the same formula:
>
> > If ... , then ... :
>
> If ... , then ... – ...   ;   if ... , then ... .
>
> Any subject is fine. Below is another example.

If you speed in Australia, then you will be fined – penalties are severe and the cops don't mess around: if you go 60 k's an hour in a school zone, then you will get zapped a $400 fine and lose four points off your license – do that three times and you lose your license for three years and have to attend a driving school (ouch!); if you go only a few k's over the limit, then there is still no mercy – you will only get a $50 fine and no points taken off, but the cops will make you feel as bad as if you've run over a granny.

We don't use such devices often. But maybe we should. If we did, we'd be able to scaffold wonderfully layered sentences, paragraphs and books. And the beauty of writing well is that even though grammar becomes unnoticeable, the power of a sentence can stay with a reader forever. Horror writer Stephen King (the inspiration behind the previous exercise) writes sentences that sweep his readers into another world, and a careful read of any of his novels reveals intricately complex sentences, some of which are pages long (King, 1981).

For more complexity, we have to go back to the Victorian writers, and the best (or worst) of these was Henry James, whose sentences baffled the world. Scan through any of his books, and you'll soon get lost in his sentences. Here's a parody of a passage from *The Turn of the Screw* (James, 1991) when the protagonist sees a ghost:

> I can't even tell you what happened that night – or rather what I saw that night (for I cannot vouch for what really happened) – except to say the darkness was profound, murky, still, and the apparition emerged and constituted itself as a face; I definitely saw it turn its head and the gesture conjured in my mind, and indeed stirred in my heart, a memory of us as lovers … the enigmatic smile she gave me therefore confirmed to me that this was she, or a ghost of what she was, in a night gown; the darkness cloaked her face and she glided slowly, in all her wonder and beauty, down the staircase and into the silence where all sense impression (and my aching heart) was lost.

Let's untangle it:

First, note the use of pairs of commas, ellipses, parentheses and dashes used to separate side comments, and explanations. Take these out, and you'll be left with the core of the sentence. The semicolons act as segment breaks.

> I can't even tell you what happened that night except to say the darkness was profound, and the apparition emerged and constituted itself as a face;
>
> I definitely saw it turn its head and the gesture conjured in my mind a memory of us as lovers …
>
> the enigmatic smile she gave me therefore confirmed to me that this was she in a nightgown;
>
> the darkness cloaked her face and she glided slowly down the staircase and into the silence where all sense impression was lost.

The sentence is still complex and makes the punctuation work hard. No minimum wages for commas here: and those usually idle parentheses and semicolons get to do some work for a change.

PAUL
I am not just trying to be obscure by writing this complex sentence. I am giving the impression of seeing a ghost, for maybe there was no ghost there. This ambiguity is carried throughout, so there is no way of telling which is the correct interpretation. I'm trying to create for the reader a sense experience, and

the sentence mirrors that impression in real time, imitating the ghost's gliding action into the darkness.

As readers we are increasingly faced with short bites of information, and need the white space, and although we tend to write to fit this trend, sometimes a long sentence can do wonders. As writers we should be able to make our sentences do marathon sprints, stop on a dime, turn corners, do magic tricks, make our readers gasp. Here's how:

> **HOW TO WRITE A COMPLEX SENTENCE EXERCISE**
>
> - Write a simple main sentence (subject-verb): *He left the room.*
>
> - Add an introductory clause: *When he noticed the looks of the patients around him,*
>
> - Add some parenthetical comments in dashes: *– they looked as if they were eating acid –*
>
> - Sandwich the main sentence with an interrupter: *he (and this was not the first time he had done this) left the room.*
>
> Result: *When he noticed the looks of the patients around him – they looked as if they were eating acid – he (and this was not the first time he had done this) left the room.*
>
> Try to avoid the pitfalls of straying into comma splices, run-ons, and fragments!

And now for some rules and how they are broken:

Rule: Don't Use Run-ons

But, is it *never* okay to use runs-ons?

> The car is barrelling down the hill faster and faster no brakes you jam your foot on the pedal harder harder but no nothing works the speedometer is edging up to 60 70 80 miles per hour and you struggle to hold the wheel turning pulling stomping on the pedal help help what can you do the mountain side whizzes by they don't call this

Deadman Pass for nothing and then you realize it's deliberate someone has cut the brakes someone wants you dead too late too late your life flashes by no the road flashes by faster faster 90 100 your little Dodge Omni has never gone so fast straining its engine and yet it goes faster and faster you're not going to make it around the next bend you hit the barrier and crash through, and you're cascading down over the pass and into the sky, floating and plummeting towards the ground close your eyes wait for the impact the last thing you see is her face.

Or fragments?

Now you know. She did it. Too late. Too late. She has your heart. Your soul. Your life. Your money. What a fool you were. Are. Will always be.

Or ellipses and dashes?

Too late ... too late ... she has your heart ... your soul ... your life ... your money ... what a fool you were ... are ... will always be.

There it is: the deliberate, breaking of rules for effect, to show, to allow the reader a visceral experience.

PAUL

Poetry too can lend itself to the use of long 'sentences'. I wrote the following poem in tribute to Allen Ginsberg's 'Howl' (1954). When I read it out loud, I soon run out of breath.

When you feel prickles all down your spine,
When some cosmic god jolts you out of alignment with time and space,
When your heart goes into arrhythmia, when you cannot breathe quite right,
When the light flashes green, and she hop hop hops onto the bike again and rides hard on the pedals to get it upright and in motion,
When she wobbles, picks up momentum and cuts through the wind, up the hill, as if she is doing her utmost to get away from you,
As if she knows you from her nightmares,
When you can fall in love with an image, with a trick of the light, with movement, colour, depth or shape, and think you are falling in love with a person,

> When you make the easy mistake of falling in love with a green dress, short brown hair, white legs pumping the pedals of an oversize boy's bike,
> Sweat on her face, down gleaming on her arm,
> Light reflecting off her bicycle handlebars,
> A million green suns behind her,
> The clumsy movements of someone trying to cope with a bike larger than she is,
> And all along you think that you are falling in love with a girl ...

These are not strictly run-on sentences. Punctuation is intact. But the sentences spill over onto the next line like rivers pouring over cliffs.

SHELLEY

My aim is to be able to turn sentences like an aerobatics pilot in command of a plane. Things might look wild and terrifying and even out of control, but underneath the barrel roll there is a guiding hand that is absolutely certain about what it's doing. I use sentence fragments and run-ons, and I sometimes start paragraphs and sentences with 'forbidden' words when I need to, with absolute intention. Like good aerobatics pilots who can make the heart of an ordinary observer stop as the plane appears to tumble out of the sky, I want to be able to harness the energy of what looks like a wild tumble and be in control of every second of that tumble.

Short Sentences

If we read long sentences for too long, we start craving a short one. Short sentences are a surprise. They offer relief. The points they make are quick and sharp. They are great for moving a plot along. They can create tension. In a sentence, rhythm is everything. And rhythm is the result of many things – among them, the length of each sentence in a paragraph.

> For example: I cannot believe what I am seeing right now. Jade. With another man. And not just another man. My brother. She looks over her shoulder. The terror in her eyes echoes the terror in mine. Then she looks at him. She quickens her pace. They quicken their pace. Mine matches theirs. Something is raging under my skin. Before I know it, I am behind them. 'Hello you two,' I say. My voice is as calm as a Sunday afternoon without traffic.

> **SHORT, SHARP SENTENCES EXERCISE**
>
> Write a 50–100 word paragraph. Keep sentences short. Choose a subject matter that lends itself to building tension such as
>
> - an attempted escape;
> - following someone;
> - staying in the shadows on a secret mission; or
> - stealing a sister's coveted chocolate bar out of the fridge.

It's good to breathe, to get relief, to vary.

Sentences can do nice tumbles too. They can imitate speech, pick up conversations, drop in raw emotions. Sentences can behave nicely and then suddenly become unruly and break all the rules, can tumble and shoot out of control. In Paul's memoir *Soldier Blue*, the writing moves along very sedately when a truck accident happens and the characters begin to panic, time speeds up, the narrative pace mirrors their tumbling thoughts:

> No, don't turn those bends so sharply – oh, it's tipping over, the whole fucken lorry is tipping over, with half the platoon helplessly strapped to the back. It's slowly falling, crushing the two mag gunners on the two corner posts. The rest wriggle free, but Bennett, the fat guy with glasses, is crushed, ballooning slowly out. My God, lift the fucken truck, you buggers! We can't, Sarge. Don't stand around, heave. Call the ambulance. They're like balloons, Sarge. I never thought people could blow out like that. The ambulance takes an hour in the hot dust. We heave and ho. Sergeant Viper curses his luck. It's happened before. In the obstacle course he threw thunderflashes and killed two recruits. He can do nothing but dust his beret and berate fate. Too bloody fast around the corners. (Williams, 2008: 150)

> **COMBINING SHORT
> AND LONG SENTENCES EXERCISE
> AND BREAKING SOME RULES**
>
> Using one of the sentences below as a prompt (if you need one), create a paragraph of 100–200 words where both short and long sentences are used for a desired effect, and in which the narrative pace at a certain point reflects the tumbling thoughts of one of the characters:
>
> *When he noticed the looks of the patients around him – they looked as if they were eating acid – he (and this was not the first time he had done this) left the room.*
>
> *Leaves rustled overhead and the moon vanished behind a cloud, and oh so quietly she crept under the sagging wire fence, her eyes focused on the shadowy form ahead.*

Spontaneous Prose

Beat poet Jack Kerouac advocates freeing the form of punctuation in sentences, and seeing sentences like musical phrases in jazz, and the writer as the jazz saxophonist.

> Kerouac: Yes, jazz and bop, in the sense of, say, a tenor man drawing a breath and blowing a phrase on his saxophone, till he runs out of breath, and when he does, his sentence, his statement's been made... that's how I therefore separate my sentences, as breath separations of the mind. (Hrebeniak, 2006: 205)

Like this, a spontaneous prose rewrite of a preceding poem:

> The first time I saw her was at the pedestrian crossing. At 1:05 every school day, a thousand boys and girls exploded through school gates into the labyrinths of purple and red pathways, but that afternoon was bruised with thunderstorms, truculent clouds rising like mushroom atomic bombs, and gnarled grandfather Jacarandas and Poinsettias clutched at kids as they cycled by, lightning crackled and spurted, the air was pungent, birds spiralled into the sky to get away, it was going to rain lions and hyenas, as it did every afternoon in December and I noticed her because she was riding a bike way too big for her, a boy's bike with the crossbar down the middle (ladies' bikes

don't have the crossbars, so the riders don't have to swing their legs immodestly over every time they mount or dismount) so she slid off one side and scuffed her brown sandal into the tarmac, she danced a short hop hop hop, her hair flew over her face, and her hat fell off and she knew I was staring at her, girls have a sixth sense when boys are gawking at them, but in that second she looked up at me, I loved her.

> **JAZZ AND BOP PROSE EXERCISE**
>
> Write a 100–200 word paragraph that uses sentences and phrases as if they are 'breath separations in the mind.' Elongate sentences; build images spontaneously, allowing them to mirror an immediate thought process.

Poetry

The first lesson about line endings is that we don't have to stop at the end of each line. The minute we discover that we can run onto the next line, poetry becomes flowing and sensuous. Punctuating poetry then can become much more interesting. There are three variations to the ending of a line: end stop, caesura and enjambment. For example:

> He stopped. She went over
> The edge and floated down.

End stop is when the sentence ends at the end of a line. Caesura is when the sentence finishes in the middle of a line. Enjambment is when the sentence flows over onto the next line.

Here is an example that plays with caesura and enjambment to create a waterfall of a poem (in honour of Gwendolyn Brooks' poem 'The Pool Players. Seven at the Golden Shovel', 1960).

> We leave home. We
> Go roam. We
> Are young. We
> Seek sun. We
> Drink Stout. We
> Run out. We
> Lose luck. We
> Get stuck.

The Souls of Sentences

William Gass maintains that sentences should have souls if they are to be alive. He is not making a theological point, but rather a poetic one:

> The sentence, then, if it is to have a soul, rather than merely be a sign of the existence somewhere of one, must be composed by our innermost being, finding in its drive and rhythm, if not in its subject, the verbal equivalent of instinct; in its sound and repetitions, too, its equivalent feeling; and then perceive its thought as Eliot and Donne did, as immediately as the odor of a rose – fully, the way we see ships at anchor rise and fall as though they lay on a breathing chest. (Gass, 1982: 65)

Sentences then do not merely point to meaning *elsewhere*: they *are* meaning, they crave to be read and spoken, and they propel stories forward in an irresistible way, like a roller coaster.

SOUL SENTENCE EXERCISE

Select at least five first sentences from bestselling novels, old classics or recent favourite reads, and ask these questions: what is the 'hook' and what pulls the reader in? What is the 'soul' in the first sentence?

Using that selection of best first sentences as an inspiration, write a single roller-coaster sentence – one that will hook readers and propel them forward.

Here is the first sentence of Paul's latest unfinished novel:

> *I have never fallen in love with a dead person before.*

Here is the first sentence of Shelley's latest unfinished memoir:

> *After twenty years, Nellie arrived at our front door just after midnight.*

Think of a sentence as a complete emotion, a direction, a state of mind, a poem entire in itself. If we write good sentences, we might put each one up on the wall, and it should stand alone as a shimmering work of art.

Powerful Paragraph Country

If sentences for William Gass have souls, then paragraphs are 'a country the eye flies over looking for landmarks, reference points, airports, restrooms, passages of sex' (Gass, 1985). A paragraph (from the Greek *paragraphos*, 'to write beside' or 'written beside') is a group of sentences with one topic. It is also a self-contained unit of a discourse in writing, dealing with a particular point or idea. A paragraph consists of one or more sentences.

So a paragraph could be pages long or made up of a sentence fragment or even only one word.

Think of paragraphs as territories or meadows, fenced off neatly, containing all we need to know within their borders. Imagine them as poems, visually pleasing to the eye. Like concrete poems, paragraphs are spatial and use white space to breathe.

Like this:

Paragraphs are the visual aesthetics of the page. When we pick up a book, if we see dense forests of text, we may be put off, or maybe we will be delighted that we can escape into them and hide for a while.

Paragraphs function as ordering blocks of argument, of topics; we create this order all the time when we write. Whether we're writing poetry, non-fiction, fiction or e-mails, we break up the information so it's palatable, easily read and noticed. We need to give readers (literal and figurative) breathing space. Page through a few books and see what effect paragraphing has on a first impression of the book. Paragraphs have a strong aesthetic impact, and there are many creative writing programmes that explicitly warn writers against too many expository chunks. The aesthetics of paragraphing are almost as important as the content. (We'll discuss this in detail in chapter 8 when we talk about what lives in the spaces between).

It's pleasing to see paragraphs.

Some are dense, sparse, one word, one-liners.

Some shout out at us. Some are slippery slopes that plunge us into tangled webs.

POWERFUL PARAGRAPH EXERCISE

Using an earlier freewrite, create two or more paragraphs out of it. Add any necessary punctuation. Break up the piece. There might be a single line that stands on its own. Feel free to experiment with the length of each paragraph.

Who knows? This could be the beginning of a future bestseller!

PAUL

A paragraph is a musical space, a graph that rises and falls, a shape. Here is a paragraph from my novel Soldier Blue, *which I wrote as a tribute to a speech by Nelson Mandela when he was sentenced to twenty-three years in jail; I also borrowed the cadences from Martin Luther King's speech written in a Birmingham jail.*

I was writing about the injustices of politics in the British colony of Rhodesia.

> What are we fighting for? For the dignity and worth of each individual, irrespective of race, colour, creed. It is a principle we are willing to die for, and one for which many have paid the ultimate price. The armed struggle is not something we have entered into lightly. But if your life is not valued as highly as a white man's dog, if you need a situpa to move from one part of your country to the other, if your first name is Kaffir and your second name Boy, if you are unable to walk on the same pavement as a white man without him spitting at you, if you have to toil on the stolen land of your ancestors to make the white man rich, if you are forced to work in the white man's mines, gardens, factories, if no one will listen to your peaceful demonstrations and pleas for humanity, if you cannot vote or have any say in the destiny of your people, if police brutality is the order of the day, if you cannot look yourself in the eye, then and only then will you understand what we are fighting for. (Williams, 2008: 73)

I was trying to build a storm here, piling thundercloud sentences up until they burst. Martin Luther King does it much, much better in his 'Letter from Birmingham Jail' (1963).

THUNDERCLOUD SENTENCE EXERCISE

Build a sentence modelled on the one above, using an emotion: anger, despair, injustice, joy. Use semicolons – and, of course, dashes – to make the point.

Here is another example from the same book, using the rhetorical device of build, build, build – break, when the protagonist mocked a girl's name. Out of her hurt, she replied to him:

Willow is the name my mother gave to me. She said that I was a tree planted on a river. No matter how rough the waters are, she said, no matter how you are whipped and snapped, no matter how badly people treat you in life, she said, you will bend, bend, bend, but you will never break. (Williams, 2008: 178)

We can think of sentences like rivers flowing. Paragraphs like meadows. Words, sentences, paragraphs – all imitate the rhythm of speech, as living conversations. If we read our words, sentences and paragraphs aloud, we can hear this rhythm. Sentences create silences, pauses, flow; they point forward, slow down and speed up as they take us on a journey, which may be a slow boat trip down a meandering river or a rollercoaster ride with sudden twists and turns. If we read pages aloud, we'll find what we talk about in the next chapter: voice.

FURTHER READING AND RELEVANT EXAMPLES

Steven Pinker's 'Grammar Puss', will free you from the anxiety of obeying grammar rules.

Read Cormac McCarthy's *The Road* to see how he uses sentence fragments for effect.

Henry James's short novel *The Turn of the Screw* is his most accessible in terms of style. Read it to see how he piles impressions upon impressions in his sentences, thereby creating ambiguity: did the governess see ghosts or not?

Stephen King's novels are full of complex sentences, as are his other writings. We took the structure of the balanced complex sentence from a paragraph in one of his short essays, 'Why We Crave Horror Movies'.

Read Allan Ginsberg's 'Howl' if you want to hear a masterful sentence in poetic form.

Jack Kerouac practised 'spontaneous writing' in his novel *On the Road*.

Gwendolyn Brooks's poem 'We Real Cool' uses enjambment to delightful effect.

Martin Luther King was a master at rhetoric, and used the sentence to powerful purpose. Read, for example, his 'Letter from Birmingham Jail' for sentences that soar and thunder.

3
Sound and Rhythm in Voice

> **Freewrite #3**
>
> *The world had never looked like this before ...*

William Gass tells us that we are doing much more than constructing sentences, paragraphs and poems when we write: 'You do not tell a story; your fiction will do that when your fiction is finished. What you make is music, and because your sounds are carriers of concepts, you make conceptual music, too' (Gass, 1977).

The mark of any great work of fiction, non-fiction or poetry is the 'voice' of the narrator. Voice can elevate a piece to greatness beyond any plot, subject or genre. Voice is ghostly, though, and nebulous. It is not located in a single word, or even a sentence. A writer's 'voice' is the most elusive element in any piece of writing. It is located in all of the narrative techniques we will discuss in this book, but also in none of them alone. So chapter 3 focuses on one of the most essential aspects of voice: the rhythm and sound of our writing and its role in creating an unforgettable original 'voice'.

PAUL

For me, my writing does not work until I have found its 'voice'. What is this mysterious thing called voice that animates a piece of writing and brings it life? The way I find voice is by playing: trying out different narrative techniques, pushing boundaries, letting characters speak out of turn, and by listening to the music of the piece. It feels instinctive: once I find the voice, I know the piece has 'got it'. It sings. It transcends its individual parts, and its words disappear.

If we can find the 'voice' in our poetry or prose, then we have uncovered the heart of the piece ... it brings our work to life. But we can easily fall into the trap of believing that we each have a single writer's voice with which we will always write, and that this is somehow the representation of who we are as writers.

A 'voice' in any piece of writing is a performance; we have many voices. In fact, as writers we are like actors: we get to try on different characters all the time, and we use varied voices in various contexts. Sometimes we rely on what we've experienced and known and what we've heard or seen either in real life or in films, and sometimes a voice comes unbidden from nowhere in particular, and we might look at our own work and think, 'I have no idea where that came from. It doesn't even sound like me.' Voice is not singular, and is the overall effect of a piece of work once we look back on it. The many voices that speak within a narrative change the tone and rhythm, shift the voice from being ironic and humorous to being full of pathos. The variations in tempo and cadence and tone are the subtle changes that make a piece either rich or poor; either a reader gets immersed in the language or skims over the words as fast as possible to get to the end of the story.

SHELLEY

I find my 'voice' in the music of whatever I'm writing – I spend more time than I'd like to admit on wrestling with the rhythm of syllables and stresses in a line, a sentence. In poetry, forms are my inspiration; in prose, I follow cadences and stresses. I've been known to completely undo a professional edit on a book that might look flawless to a casual reader, because in the rearranging of words, my voice has disappeared and suddenly I feel as though my work has been hijacked by aliens! I'm inspired by writers whose voices compel me to identify with unique states of being and experiences.

So let's begin with the score, with the music and rhythm behind the language we use. Our fictional characters all need voices, as does the narrative itself. Every poem, story, novel or non-fiction book needs a voice. The rhythm of language is the underlying beat to a piece and is the invisible thread that joins together all the elements of the later entity that will become the writer's voice.

Accents, Syllables and Stress

Sometimes we fall in love with a particular accent. We may love the way BBC English broadcasters say 'annoying' or the way West Coast Americans say 'Oregon'. We may love Italian English accents, or French English accents for the sheer pleasure we take in the way certain words fall into the world. We may equally have an aversion to what certain accents do to certain words. The interesting thing is, that most of us have some kind of emotional reaction to the way others pronounce words!

SHELLEY

I will admit to reacting with some feeling (often annoyance!) to the way people use language sometimes. Having lived in different English-speaking countries all over the world, I've developed some allergies to certain expressions and fallen in love with others. I love how Americans say, 'I don't give a rat's ass.' It sounds so superbly dismissive. In America, though, I heard people saying, 'All the sudden' instead of 'all of a sudden'. The Mispronunciation and Expression Police honestly need to ensure that offenders, once caught, are taught and then made to promise never to make such an error again! I was teaching at a primary school and the kids would often say, 'I did it on accident,' to which I'd reply like some irate nineteenth-century governess: 'By accident. On purpose.' In Australia, when I first arrived, some of the expressions took me completely by surprise and seemed hilarious: 'Bloody ripper, mate,' just means, 'That's awesome.' The Mispronunciation Police are needed in Australia too, where people say the letter 'h' as 'haitch', as in, 'I'm doing my Pee Haitch Dee!' I'm pretty sure that pronunciation originated in England, as did the habit of ending a sentence with the word but as if it were the word though, as in: 'He liked the ice-cream, but.' Some expressions and pronunciations just get under some people's skin for reasons that may be deep and profound or superficial and petty. Anyway, we will never be able to make everyone speak in ways that satisfy our own sense of aesthetics, but if we listen to the sound and rhythm of conversations around us, we can be inspired by even the things that annoy us, and infuse our writing with the richness of all kinds of expression.

The sounds of words, where the accent falls, what each writer loves, is the important aspect of this chapter. Whether we are writers of poetry or prose, the music of words, the number of syllables and where stress falls create the rhythm in our writing and ultimately lead to 'voice'.

And if we listen to the sarcastic, funny, ironic, serious conversations on the bus, the train, at cafes, in school, at work and hear how people speak, how they tell stories, our own telling and writing becomes enriched.

Alliterative verse, which we find in its formal glory in old English poems such as *Beowulf*, enables us to find and use words we may never have thought of, and so images evolve that we may not have known lived in us. The example below, though not strictly in the style of *Beowulf*, relies on two alliterative words at the start of the line (words that begin with the same consonant) and two at the end, to create its rhythm. A voice emerges out of the form that the writer may never have otherwise been able to consciously construct.

Here's an example:

Think Thin

*Shelley-Shoes, when will you
Start slimming that big bum?*

*Thin at thirteen, fat at fourteen
faded at fifteen, sick by sixteen
counting calories, dreaming dog food
think thin, says the Pretend Princess.
Food's fatal, I wield willpower
beyond belief. I don't need nourishment –
no one scorns a skinny skeleton.*

Slowly sickening, we die daily,
deprived daughters with thin thighs.

SHELLEY

I wrote this poem in my thirties, looking back on my anorexic teenage self. Without the alliterative form, I don't know that my ideas would have emerged as they did. Using this particular alliterative form jogged my memory: it took me back to my teens and a stupid fridge magnet I'd bought that said 'Think Thin', a constant reminder not to open the fridge door!

As I sat down to write my poem, what instantly came to mind was the kind of sentence one never forgets, least of all because it was alliterative: the father of a close friend of mine always called me 'Shelley-Shoes' and thought he was funny, constantly asking me when I was going to lose some weight off my big bum! I felt foul! Hello, anorexia! Anyway, form creates content. I love that.

ALLITERATIVE ACTION EXERCISE

1. Write a poem of 10–12 lines. Each line should have four alliterative words; all four can share the same alliterative sound, or they can be divided into two sets of two, as in 'Think Thin'. There can be a pause between the first set of alliterative words and the second.

2. Write a poem of 10–12 lines that has three alliterative words per line. There can be a pause between the first two words and the last one, as in 'Unwritten Poems' below.

These build on the associative word exercises, as the form demands a search for alliterative words that may otherwise not have come to mind.

The poem below is similar – an accentual written for the Poultry Group that relies on three alliterative words per line:

Unwritten Poems

Bunched into old nursing bras, bright thoughts
Are dispersed into the dryer. Our dishwasher
Secretes word sequences, whole stanzas
On lost loves and latitudes.
I make memories, then mill them in
A coffee grinder – (visions crush quickly to caffeine).
I search for shards of images sucked
Into the vibrating void of the vacuum cleaner,
Disturbed to discover only dust and dirt.
I wonder if my son will wake
To find the one I folded flat
Into his Panda pyjamas – a long poem
Lost one night, late in the laundry.

Repetition and Refrains

Rhythm and alliteration are the soul of potent prose. If we think of each sentence like a line of poetry, we can become aware of the power of the rhythm in each line and make prose work with the same power as poetry. Repetition is a powerful tool too for creating voice. In both poetry and prose, repetition creates a certain rhythm. As we know, if a letter is repeated, we get alliteration or assonance. But if a word or phrase is repeated, we get refrains, which have a certain mesmerizing power and create a certain style or voice.

In any paragraph, the repetition of a word amplifies its significance. This works in prose as well as poetry.

> *I love chocolate. I have always loved chocolate. I would die without chocolate. And any chocolate will do. Hot chocolate. White chocolate. Chocolate fudge. Chocolate cereal. You should see me when I don't get my daily fix. You should see me when I do get my daily fix. Choc-o-late! Chocolate!*

A repeated phrase in a paragraph could be poetically very powerful.

> *I don't want to go to bed! He accented each word with his fist on the table. He gave his fiercest stare. He kicked her under the table. I don't want to go to bed!*

You need to stop
You worked all year on the house. You worked all day on your body. You worked all year on your car.
You need to stop.
You pursued me all month. You sent me flowers, you sent me chocolates, you called me, you texted me.
You need to stop.
Now.

> **REPETITION EXERCISE**
>
> Write a paragraph that includes a repeated word or phrase using the examples above as a point of departure.

Rhythm: The Writer's Beat

Iambic pentameter is a common rhythm in Shakespeare's sonnets and in villanelles and other poetic forms. Although the odd rhythm of the iambic pentameter feels disconcerting at first because it doesn't follow the regular 4/4 timing of, for example, ballad poetry, pentameter with its five beats imitates regular speech. Writing in iambic pentameter (and using blank verse like Shakespeare often did) can lead to surprising results and create a specific voice. An iamb is an unstressed syllable followed by a stressed syllable. Five iambs in a row make a line of iambic pentameter (*pent* means 'five' in Greek, as in *pentagon* or *pentathlon*). Each line has ten syllables, five stressed and five unstressed, as in the poem below:

Before the Desert

Before the windswept shifting sands and plains
Before the silence of the womenfolk,
There was a river – music over rocks
Which fed a fertile valley, rich and green.
When women's voices lifted into song
Their soft vibrating tones loosed water from
High elevations; sent it rushing down
To nourish those who worked the fruitful land.
But then a harsh and thankless violent hand

Brought silence down, and water ceased to flow.
Men shouted, fought, trailed murder in their wake
And women's silence as the desert grew –
A hundred thousand acres in a year.

SHELLEY

This poem was the result of a dream I had just before we went to live and teach in the Middle East. The voice is the result of using iambic pentameter, which forces the choice of certain words over others and creates a mood, a narrator's persona, a particular tone, which matches the subject matter. The rhythm is supposed to reflect the movement of time and history now shaping a current reality.

> **IAMBIC PENTAMETER EXERCISE**
>
> Write a poem of 10–12 lines that uses iambic pentameter (ten syllables in each line). The first syllable of each line should be unstressed.
>
> See what emerges when there is a restriction on syllables, and how each line begins.

The Voice of the Villanelle

In popular music, the refrain or repeated line of the song gives it power and may even change its meaning as the song progresses.

One of the best ways to experience the power of repetition and its role in creating voice is to write a villanelle. The villanelle emerged as a type of pastoral song in France in the 1600s; it eventually evolved into its current form and has been well used by many poets over the ages.

The form is fixed: nineteen lines in total, comprised of five tercets (three lines) and a quatrain (four lines), with lines repeated throughout. The line repetitions are what make villanelles so surprising and often profound. Because the repeated lines are sometimes at the beginning, middle or end of a stanza, their context changes. It's exactly as if someone put on a bright red T-shirt and stood in front of a green screen. Then, imagine that person changed the screen to black, then blue and finally to yellow. The combination of red with each of these colours would give the red a new context, a new relationship, an entirely different meaning:

I long for spring – my heart resists the cold
A writer, like a flower, needs the sun.
The winter speaks of sighs and growing old.

I walk the windy beach in wool and fold
My hands inside my sleeves. I try to run –
I long for spring – my heart resists the cold.

I left my country where the light was gold
And travelled north to hide from those with guns.
The winter speaks of sighs and growing old.

I never learned the art of being bold
I left my home; my soul-threads came undone.
I long for spring – my heart resists the cold.

The words, the stories, every tale I've told
Transports me back to land from whence I've come
The winter speaks of sighs and growing old.

An icy blast puts every thought on hold
Except this poem, which I've somehow won.
I long for spring, my heart resists the cold
The winter speaks of sighs and growing old.

ADVENTUROUS VILLANELLE EXERCISE

Here is how you do it:

1. Number 19 lines down a page, with a gap after lines 3, 6, 9 and 12.
2. Write a line of iambic pentameter (a line with ten syllables or five beats. Accents.) This is your *Refrain 1*.
3. Cut and paste this line onto lines 1, 6, 12 and 18.
4. Write another line that rhymes with this line, and cut and paste it onto lines 3, 9, 15 and 19. This is your *Refrain 2*.
5. Now fill in the sandwich (lines 2, 5, 7, 8, 11, 14 and 17) with lines that rhyme with each other, but not with your other refrains.
6. Write the final line (16) rhyming with your first refrains.
7. Voilà!

Punctuating Prose and the Creation of Voice

William Gass tells us that we create music through our words. Then Theodor Adorno goes further and suggests that the music is created in our punctuation:

> There is no element in which language resembles music more than in the punctuation marks. The comma and the period correspond to the half-cadence and the authentic cadence. Exclamation points are punctuation marks like silent cymbal clashes, question marks like musical upbeats, colons dominant seventh chords; and only a person who can perceive the different weights of strong and weak phrasings in musical form can really feel the distinction between the comma and the semicolon. (Adorno, 1990: 300–1)

If voice is the rhythm and sound and music of our writing, then the instruments we use to produce this music are the words, sentences, paragraphs. In the examples below we harness the mechanics of punctuation for its greater purpose: music, cadence or voice.

Example:

> Jade was always the centre of attention. She was bewitching. She was intelligent. She was a great listener.

or

> Jade: always at the centre – bewitching, intelligent, she was a great listener.

or

> Jade – the centre of attention: bewitching, intelligent, and a great listener.

MUSICAL PROSE EXERCISE

Rephrase and re-punctuate these sentences to achieve a haunting and powerful cadence. Play with punctuation until the desired effect is achieved:

> *Jonathan was on his way to school. He saw a starving dog whose ribs stuck out. The dog wandered across the road. The dog did not see the oncoming van.*

PAUL

When I am expressing an emotion, say anger, or self-pity, my sentences lengthen, and the writing piles up indignant images one on top of the other:

> All she had ever wanted was silence. But her teen years were punctuated by dogs, mowers, blowers, the motorway; all she smelled was the nearby tip; in winter smoke from all the fires choked the air; in summer, quad bikes tore up the reserve. Nature for men (all men, there were no exceptions) was a place to dump rubbish, to scramble bikes, to saw and blow and mulch and mow: the silence was there to be filled. Heaven forbid there should be quiet or peace!

When I want to reflect a burst of emotion, of affection, I use repetition, sentences that beat in the rhythm of a pulsing heart. The following story is about a creative writing teacher. The piece builds to a crescendo – punctuation helps the sentences move faster as they graduate from full stops to semicolons to commas. The whole musical piece is framed by two short sentence 'book ends':

> He likes his students. He likes the sincere policeman who hates arresting people, who has taken creative writing because he wants to feed his soul. He likes the woman with the big buckteeth who with a two-year-old son breaks his heart because she has had her heart broken by a series of unscrupulous men who have taken advantage of her; he likes the enthusiasm of the photography student with braces and an ambition to be a horror writer like Stephen King, the Danish student whose boyfriend is in Afghanistan, whose stories she writes from his point of view, the home schooled sixteen-year-old boy who comes out of the closet in his stories, daring to have fictional homo-erotic relationships, but never real ones. The seventy-three-year-old woman who cannot hear, the miner who has black fingernails, the man who brings two Cokes to class, the Indian woman who smiles all through the class, the woman who hides behind a wall of make-up ... . And they in turn give him hugs, presents, write him emails with hearts and smiley faces. Valentine cards. They love him.

For centuries musical composers have been echoing their predecessors, their contemporaries. Certain elements of style are always a given so that we can identify the distinctive features of a baroque piece or a classical piece or twentieth-century music. And we do this with writing as well. As writers we often echo the voices of others, either consciously or unconsciously.

SHELLEY

In my memoir, The Eye of the Moon, *I was deeply influenced by the poetic quality found in the work of writers Marguerite Duras, Jean Rhys and Shirley Hazzard. What emerged after my submersion in their voices was, of course, my own voice, but my rhythm and phrasing owes something to the poetry of their language. I wrote an African memoir, and the voice was quite unlike any other I have ever used, and probably unlike the voices that influenced me, which is what happens because a writer's voice is as unique as an individual fingerprint. It is something written into the deepest parts of ourselves, I think. The voice in my memoir emerged from the rhythm, as if I was writing an extended poem:*

> Branches litter the riverbank from the summer floods some months before, and the sun is bright in a harsh and merciless sky. This is where we meet. Secretly. I wait for him behind the tree and he drives up in a gold Toyota automatic. It's the car they share.
>
> The Toyota is dusty from the wheels up. The gold doors are splashed with hardened mud. Winter, in this part of South Africa, is brief and dry. The veld turns to gold and night after night, fires light up the horizons, fires that turn the ground to black and the air to gray. In the mornings, skeletons of small animals lie scattered across the burnt earth and the smell of ash and decay is bitter in the wind. (Davidow, 2007: 1)

IN THE FOOTSTEPS OF THE MASTERS (AND MISTRESSES) EXERCISE

Find a paragraph (or two) written by a favourite writer whose prose and rhythm and style are inspiring. The piece can be humorous, serious, sarcastic or poignant.

1. Copy the paragraph word for word (preferably with a pen on paper), feeling what it's like to *be* this writer, to write that way. Notice things about his or her style, the technique that creates voice.

2. Now write a paragraph (any subject matter) that echoes the rhythm and cadences of the previous copied paragraph.

(This exercise can, of course, be repeated with many writers as literary examples.)

Exercises in imitation are great practice. Just as brilliant artists and composers start off emulating great teachers, so we can start off learning by echoing the patterns and beats of voices we admire. When we imitate a style, a voice, we're learning explicitly and implicitly about voice. We're inhabiting a genre, a style, and even though we may think we are starting to sound just like the original, we will still unavoidably be creating our own unique narrative voice. All through the ages, young apprentices studied with masters, worked on their music, their art and their philosophies, and gained skills. The philosopher Aristotle was the student of the master Plato, who was the student of the doomed but courageous Socrates; and even as the students learned from their teachers, they became themselves, found their own pathways, stood on the shoulders of those who had gone before and came up with their own voices in the world, their own narratives and ideas.

Looking back at literature through the ages, finding writers whose voices we can admire, who lived in different times and responded to different social milieus, reading their words and writing our own in response, all this supports us on our writing journey so that ultimately our own voice, if we let it, will emerge, liberated, completely and uniquely ours.

We have an 'anthology of selves' inside us. Every act of writing is a 'performance of self' and an opportunity to be those unique selves.

INSPIRING EXAMPLES

For syllabic poetry, read *Beowulf* or *Sir Gawain and the Green Knight*.

For iambic pentameter, read Shakespeare!

Great examples of villanelles: Elizabeth Bishop's 'One Art'; Dylan Thomas's 'Do Not Go Gentle into That Good Night'; Wendy Cope's 'Lonely Hearts'.

For inspiring poetic prose read Arundhati Roy's *The God of Small Things*, Marguerite Duras's *The Lover*, Jean Rhys's *The Wide Sargasso Sea* or Shirley Hazzard's *The Transit of Venus*.

4
Angling for a View – Who's Telling?

> **Freewrite #4**
>
> *She rushed through the thousands, pushing everyone out of the way ...*

We are all storytellers. Every day of our lives we are telling someone something about something. We are, in essence, narrative creatures. Our brains are fine-tuned for it. We love it. Living without it would be near impossible. Sit for five minutes in a coffee shop on a Sunday morning and listen to the air – it is frantic with narratives tumbling over each other, some true, some truly made up, some poetic. Whether we're telling a friend about the discovery of an earthlike planet in a distant solar system or gossiping about another friend's dubious affair, no listener really cares about anything except whether the narrative is interesting.

And how we as writers hold the interest of a listener or reader is with our narrative voice. It's a skill to be able to craft the identity of the teller of our narratives – to put that teller in the appropriate position.

We've learned how to mesmerize readers by the rhythm and repetition that makes up the essential scaffolding for building voice. But ultimately, voice is non-local – it is the effect of a whole piece. And though none of us may like to admit it, even in our everyday telling of Sunday morning narratives, our 'voice' changes. If we talk to a two-year-old about a plane, or a seventeen-year-old about global warming, or a close friend about an embarrassing event, the narrative voices we use are distinctive depending on what the story is and who's listening. So our narrative position is totally unique to each particular narrative and its audience.

Some narratives seem to tell themselves without any help, but of course that's a literary illusion which any practised writer can pull off. The identity of that telling voice could be anyone, even the author herself, wryly hiding behind a narrator. It could be a character in a story confessing to us, the readers. The storyteller could be a bystander, (Nick Carraway in *The Great Gatsby*) or the main protagonist (Huck in *The Adventures of Huckleberry Finn*). Sometimes the reader is unaware of the distant, aloof, Godlike narrator who sees all and makes snooty judgements on the mortals she portrays. In non-fiction, the narrator is the author's voice and is still a careful construct. Any reader knows that a parenting book written in a dry know-it-all voice is a lost cause.

Often the narrator in fiction or poetry is a shadowy character who is invisible, not identified – someone elusive who obviously doesn't go to the toilet or get stomach cramps or headaches, and doesn't get in the way of the story. Sometimes the narrator is the main character, and we can hear that voice, especially if we read these passages aloud. And on occasion, a narrator intrudes in a narrative and makes us aware of the very nature of its construction.

PAUL

I often struggle to find the 'voice' in my fiction. I can have the plot and characters, but the story is dead until it gets a voice. I have to play around until I hit it. I tinker with first, second and third person points-of-view, narrators, story positioning, and encourage quirky off-the-wall insights. Sometimes a phrase someone says in passing helps; sometimes I have to try out character voices and let them tell me which one works. In spite of its mystical intangibility, as we discussed in the last chapter, voice can be engineered and constructed, and there are techniques for getting it. Some of those include plundering, trying on, appropriating and inhabiting other voices.

But, as a contradiction, voice comes when we are being ourselves, being honest as writers. Even as we create diverse points of views, characters and lives, a reader can detect a phoney voice miles away.

Film narratives emerged from written ones, which emerged from the oral tradition. When movies came along, they located the position of the narrator explicitly. The camera placed the viewer and the narrator in a particular relationship, and since then written narratives have learned a lot from film. Here's a correlation between perspectives in film and written narratives: if a film opens with a scene where we are looking at a train with a person inside holding a balloon and hugging his suitcase, it's the equivalent of the close third-person point of view. If we're flying high over the landscape, so high that we can see a car driving down a singular road that leads to an intersection in the middle of nowhere, the narrative is from the point of view of the omniscient third person. If the camera is just over the shoulder of a character and we are being made to identify with the character, we're in the narrative equivalent of a second-person point of view. When we're the eyes of this character, looking out through the window at the middle of nowhere, we, the viewers, are in the first-person perspective.

In fiction, poetry and non-fiction, our narrative positioning gives our work its uniqueness: point of view results in the effective construction of irony, of humour, of confessional intimacy or omniscient transcendence.

It's My Story and I'm Telling It: First-person Perspective

In a way, first person is the most natural point of view to use in narrative (poetry and fiction) because this is how we speak, and we can pour all we know into that point of view (even if it's all made up). And sometimes, writing as an 'I' can be the first step to overcoming writer's block.

But as soon as we put pen to paper (or finger to plastic keyboard), the 'I' becomes a narrator, a persona. The 'I' of a story or poem is *never* the writer behind the story, even in a memoir or autobiography; the first-person narrator is always a construct, a character in a parallel writer's universe.

Advantages of the first-person point of view (POV) are obvious: a reader gets insight into how the character thinks. As writers we can present intimate internal thoughts and feelings and confessions. The voice is easy to identify. But this is also a disadvantage: we can end up 'telling' the story rather than 'showing' our readers what's happening, which is fine when the narrator is confessing things to an eager reader, but tricky in terms of holding a long and involved plot together. Another (maybe contradictory) disadvantage is that it is difficult for the reader to *see* the first-person narrator. Literally, we see everything through her eyes, so only if a device like a mirror is used can a reader actually see her, unless a friend conveniently drops in and says, 'Gee, your long brown hair is so shiny today, and how did you get that bruise?'

In the following example (another supermarket checkout story) we get an insight into a quirky personality's thoughts and feelings, but we don't get to see what he looks like or how old he is, although we can make some assumptions because of what he knows and the language he uses:

> Good morning, how has your day been? Let me take those for you, ma'am. Any Reward card? You want cash out? I can hear myself.

I have said this to a hundred and fifty customers today, yet the smile is still fixed on my face, cheesy and it fools them, hey it fools me, act happy and you'll be happy. Forget the ache in my lower back from standing for three hours. Whiz the purchases across the scanner, damn I hate the fruit I can't even recognize this. Is it a pomegranate? Beep beep beep. Pling. You qualify for school dinosaur stickers. Beep beep. I think it's a C note or a C#. I have perfect pitch, you know, and here I am smiling at a line of impatient, sour krauts. You want the meat separate? Your eggs are here, sir.

> **CHARACTER EXPOSÉ EXERCISE**
>
> Write an account from the first-person point of view (100–200 words) of an event. Allow the narrative to reveal the character, the way he or she thinks, how old the person might be and what this individual is doing.

This is a straight first-person account. But there is another position the first person can hold, one that's not quite reliable.

I'm Telling, but Don't Believe Everything I Say: The Unreliable First Person

Readers are quickly and easily sucked into the point of view of a first-person narrator. There is an unspoken contract of trust between reader and author. But some narrators break the contract (on purpose). And for effect. The reader is put on edge, compelled to read further because there's a disturbing discrepancy between the narrator's telling and what the reader knows. The position makes for interesting narratives.

PAUL

At eleven years old I read The Adventures of Huckleberry Finn *(the unabridged version). It was a challenge for me, but I loved particularly the voice, or voices, Mark Twain had constructed, using various dialects, particularly the first-person confessional. Huck was directly talking to me. And promised that his story would be the truth, and not 'stretchers' (lies). But as the novel progressed, I began to realize that something was wrong. His version of reality was not mine – he was getting it wrong. He sweated over his guilty conscience because he was doing a 'terrible' thing, freeing a slave. And later in the novel, he took aboard his raft two scamming rogues but believed they were an English King and Duke. I (as reader) could see he was being hoodwinked, but he could not. The novel danced between the first-person narrator's version of truth and my own.*

Here is a story from the point of view of a seriously unreliable narrator, a tribute to a famous poem by a famous poet:

> There we sat, her lovely head on my shoulder, in front of the fire. 'Comfy, my love?' I murmured, and when she said nothing, I stroked her soft hair and pressed my lips against her cold cheek. I opened her eyelids and gazed into her eyes. She was mine at last. She loved me now. I unfastened the tie around her neck, touched the bruises that were beginning to swell her throat, and propped her head up against me. Pressed her cold hands in mine.

PAUL
I took this idea from Victorian poet Robert Browning's unreliable first person in his narrative poem, 'Porphyria's Lover'. At first we are taken in by his love making, and then in horror realize that he is cradling a corpse in front of his fireplace!

UNRELIABLE FIRST-PERSON EXERCISE

Write a first-person confession (100–200 words) that gains the reader's initial trust. Then make the narrative unreliable by revealing things that point to the fact that the narrator is not seeing things the way they really are.

He Stepped onto the Train: An Objective Third-person Account

Imagine a camera following a character from above. The young man has just boarded a train in London. We can see him yawn, rub his eyes, but we have no interior access to his thoughts or feelings except what shows on his face and what reveals itself through movements, actions and dialogue. This is objective third person. It also parallels how we perceive the world. We can only understand other people by what we perceive of their behaviour. In life, we often only have our observations of the world to guide our assumptions and intuitions about others. And in writing, less is often more. The reader is shown what is going on, and the messages and themes emerge in the subtext, in what we read into things unsaid. Ernest Hemingway is a master of this technique. Read any of his short stories, for example 'Hills Like White Elephants,' and the objective third person works to simply describe, and not comment on what is seen and heard.

Here is an example of a scene told by a detached narrator:

> He arrived at five on a Sunday morning, tumbled through the mazes of the underground, dragged his suitcase with the broken handle along interminable tunnels of concrete. At the bottom of a long escalator at Victoria Station he stumbled across a knot of men and women at the tail end of an all-night party. Each carried a pink and silver heart-shaped balloon. He tried to slide past but a large man with a wide grin handed him a balloon, with HAPPY BIRTHDAY FRANK printed on the one side in confetti and glitter.
>
> 'Who's Frank?' he said.
>
> 'You are. Happy birthday, Frank.'
>
> He took the balloon, pushed past the crowd, and into a Victoria train. He clutched the string tight, and the balloon bobbed against the roof of the carriage. A woman opposite stared, a smile curling on her face. He closed his eyes, but every time he opened them, she was staring at him. Smiling. 'Happy birthday, Frank,' she mouthed silently.
>
> He nodded. 'Thank you.' (Williams, 2011)

'LESS IS MORE' EXERCISE: OBJECTIVE THIRD PERSON

Write a paragraph using the freewrite prompt at the beginning of this chapter as a starting point, if it helps. Describe only what the outside observer would see. The objective third person camera follows this character. The camera has no access to the internal thoughts of the character.

She Wished He Would Stop Staring: Close Third-person Point of View

A distant camera moves in closer. Sometimes it's located in the mirror that a character stares into. This allows the viewer to see everything from the protagonist's point of view in the close third-person position.

A viewer can even be inside her head. At the same time, though, the angle allows the viewer to see the character as others might – her hair, the way the light falls on her face, her gestures. The close third person is internal and external at once, and romance authors love it.

Here's an example:

> Addie was twenty-two, a history student at the University of Hull, fiercely independent, anti-male, anti-anything; slim; pale, very English, and in love with Australia. Well, the idea of Australia. All her friends had done the obligatory clichéd tour down under: Byron Bay, the Rocks, Uluru, Great Barrier Reef. No, not that Australia. She wanted to get under the glossy skin of the country. To throw herself into something unusual.
>
> She had the hell in with her life here in Hull, with the grey non-weather, the absence of an economy, her parents, her brother, her appenditious boyfriend, and most of all the pretentious university courses that were leading nowhere except to inflate lecturers' egos. She was tired of wearing black, tired of smoking all day. She was tired of being this self that had formed around her like an invisibility cloak.

In this story, we could easily be fooled into thinking the narrator is Addie herself, as this is close third person. It's evident that we are in the character's head for most of that passage, except that we can see her from the outside as well. The question is, would this passage work as easily in the first person, and would it make any difference? Out of interest, let's give it a try:

> I was twenty-two, a history student at the University of Hull, fiercely independent, anti-male, anti-anything; slim; pale, very English, and in love with Australia. Well, the idea of Australia. All my friends had done the obligatory clichéd tour down under: Byron Bay, the Rocks, Uluru, Great Barrier Reef. No, not that Australia. I wanted to get under the glossy skin of the country. To throw myself into something unusual.
>
> I had the hell in with my life here in Hull, with the grey non-weather, the absence of an economy, my parents, my brother, my appenditious boyfriend, and most of all the pretentious university courses that were leading nowhere except to inflate lecturers' egos. I was tired of wearing black, tired of smoking all day. I was tired of being this self that had formed around me like an invisibility cloak.

That's awkward: Addie is cringingly self-conscious, objectifying herself. The narrator's position is inconsistent with the rules of a first-person point of view, which is that the first person cannot see herself from the outside.

> **OVER-THE-SHOULDER, CLOSE THIRD-PERSON EXERCISE**
>
> Write a paragraph (100–200 words) from the close, third-person point of view. Use the third-person paragraph about Addie as a guide, or look at the first paragraph of a few romance novels; chances are they will be using the close third-person point of view.

You're Happy and You Know it: The Ubiquitous Second Person

Many writing coaches and teachers advise against using the second person. 'Use any other form of narration but straight first- or third-person', says John Braine, 'and you'll be wasting your time. You may even risk a worse fate than rejection, which is not to finish the novel' (Braine, 2000: 119).

PAUL

I beg to differ. Second-person narrative, though peculiar and unsettling, is sometimes necessary. We use second-person narration all the time. If someone asks for directions, you say: 'You'll want to make a left here, then go straight on.' Or cooking: 'Stir the sauce; beat the eggs, and then voilà, it's done.' The implied you. But in fiction it may feel rude to command your reader what to do. It can also feel affected and self-conscious.

The first draft of my novel Cokcraco *was written using a first-person point of view. I wrote the whole book and by the time I finished, I just knew there was something 'wrong' with the voice:*

> I'm driving down a red dirt road in the middle of South Africa, having turned off at the intersection of nowhere and nowhere. I'm lost.

The novel didn't work because I needed some distance (not too much) from the narrator. So I tried the objective third person, with its potential for critical distance, and rewrote the whole book, changing things here and there so that I didn't end up with an awkwardly close third-person point of view:

> He is driving down a red dirt road in the middle of South Africa, having turned off at the intersection of nowhere and nowhere. He's lost.

That too just didn't do it. I wanted to invite the reader in, to say, 'Hey, this is how it feels to be the protagonist of the story.' I wanted, I admit, an edge, to be in your face. But we're all warned about writing in the second person, about making the reader into the protagonist. As a writer, you are cursed to fail before you even begin. But I had no choice. In the third draft, I changed the point of view to second person, and the moment I did it, something clicked into place:

> You're driving down a red dirt road in the middle of South Africa, having turned off at the intersection of nowhere and nowhere. You're lost. You're late for a meeting. The aircon in the rental car doesn't work, and you're wearing a European suit. You should stop and ask for directions, but you're male, genetically programmed never to ask for directions. (Williams, 2013: 1)

The book is a very different animal in second person. First person felt too selfishly enclosed, third too distant. The second person inadvertently got the book into the 'Goldilocks Zone', where the reader was positioned just right and the voice could speak its truth.

But it is a game, of course. You, the reader, cannot be the protagonist unless it's a computer game. In a novel, you are being ordered about, and it's not you; it's another character. In Cokcraco, *'you' is not the reader at all, but the white male protagonist who is experiencing life in South Africa as an alien. But you, the reader, are forced into a role of identification with the protagonist that is sandwiched neatly between first and third person.*

GOLDILOCKS EXERCISE: FIRST TO SECOND, TO THIRD PERSON

1. Write a short paragraph (50–100 words) in the first person.
2. Now rewrite it in the third person.
3. Next, try writing the same piece in the second person.

Where does the 'Goldilocks Zone' lie for that particular piece, and which point of view gives the piece the voice that you want?

PAUL

Be careful of switching viewpoints in a piece. In an early version of Cockraco, *I hadn't done a fine edit, and the result was a book peppered with these kinds of errors:*

> *I closed his eyes, and could feel the sticky liquid run down his throat. (!!!)*

The narrator is key to the voice of the story, showing us how to listen, revealing what we need to know, or maybe confusing us, as unreliable narrators do, so that we have to construct the story in spite of the narrator.

Unique Angles in Space: Moving Narrators into Adjacent Territories

Most of us will already know how to use and write from the previous points of view, at least to some degree, but there are many different positions for our narrators to occupy, which can result in our voices becoming increasingly innovative or sophisticated. So let's look at some of the more unique angles or points of view:

Being the All-knowing, All-seeing Omniscient Creator (Who Is Everywhere at All Times)

The omniscient (all knowing), third-person, God's point of view was a very popular convention in Victorian fiction. Society had a worldview that was secure. Or at least pretended very well that this was the case. Truth was evident. A narrator could wide-angle the scene, then zoom into a tight close-up of someone's internal feelings, then jump immediately into another person's thoughts and then comment on his or her opinions on these characters.

Like this:

> Gerald knew he should not go back to the house, but he felt a premonition. Foolish man. Little did he realize that Georgina was waiting for him, with her poisonous agenda. She could not bear to think of life without him, so had plotted to hide his keys, knowing that when he couldn't find them, he'd come trotting back. Vain, arrogant, futile. For Gerald had seen through her scheme and was returning only to score a victory.

The narrator knows all. Most common today is a variation on this theme – the use of multiple points of view in segments – fractured third-person slivers that make up a jigsaw puzzle. Thrillers build up tension this way and use this device to give multiple perspectives, but without the judgement. We accept these consecutive points of view readily in movies where the viewer can be shifted radically from one character and scene to another without saying, 'Hey, wait a minute. Whose point of view are we in now?'

> **THE ALL-KNOWING CREATOR EXERCISE**
>
> Create a wide-angle view of a scene (200 words) in which you zoom into a third-person close-up of someone's internal feelings and then jump immediately into another person's thoughts, and then (being the all-knowing creator that you are) you make a comment or reveal an opinion on these characters. Use the Gerald and Georgina passage as a template.

Narrators Who Aren't There, and Epistolary Texts

Here's a question: can there *ever* be a story without a narrator?

Stephen King's *Carrie* is a series of newspaper clippings and reports. As far as we can see, no narrator exists to guide us. We, as readers, become the narrator. This epistolary form uses multiple and varied voices to tell its story. The narrator takes a back seat and lets the reader construct the meaning, fill in the gaps. James Joyce (Irish writer, early twentieth century) suggested that it should seem as though the author (and perhaps the narrator) shows little interest in the story: 'The artist, like the God of the creation, remains within or behind or beyond or above his handiwork, invisible, refined out of existence, indifferent, paring his fingernails' (Joyce, 1994: 233).

The first novels in English in the eighteenth century were epistolary: think Jane Austen and the extensive use of letters from one character to another. The epistolary text can take other forms too. It could be a diary, a journal or a series of newspaper articles, emails or text messages. Graffiti, skywriting – all of these devices convey messages, usually from one character to another. Along the way the messages reveal information. We could create a whole book that is epistolary, without any 'voice' except the ones that emerge from the letters or diary entries. More often, though, this form is a device used within another kind of narrative.

With an absent narrator, there's no one watching. The reader (outside the text) becomes a voyeur eavesdropping on private communications within the narrative. Epistolary narratives can be monologic (one character's voice), dialogic (two characters' voices) or polylogic (numerous voices). Discrepant awareness is the result: the outside reader is aware of shifts in meaning between what might be revealed in a diary, for example, and what the news report might say that night.

SHELLEY

The fun thing about epistolary texts is that as a writer I get to inhabit other points of view. It is such a great escape to look at the world through other eyes for a while. Below is a polylogic example from my speculative young adult novel Lights Over Emerald Creek.

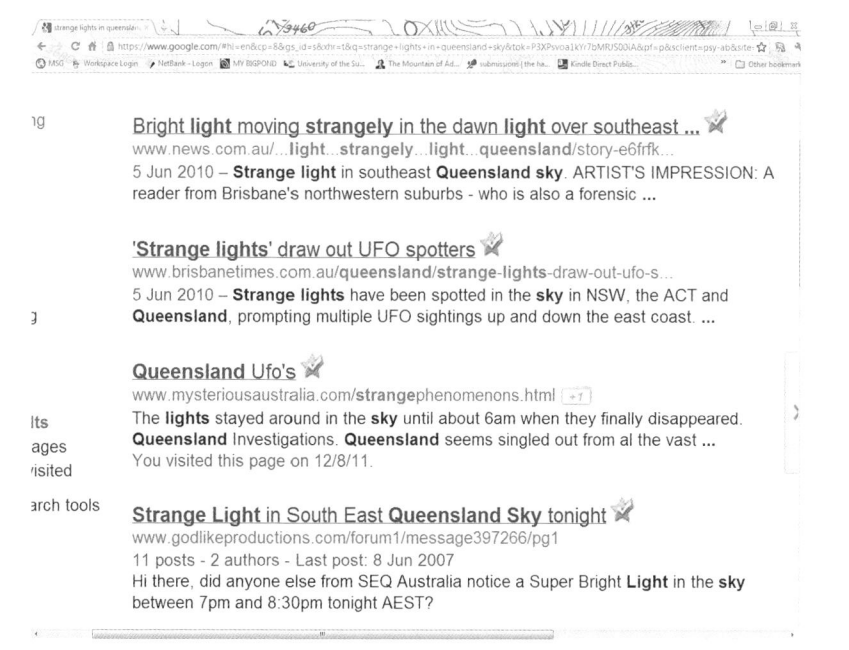

Bright light moving strangely in the dawn light over southeast ...
www.news.com.au/...light...strangely...light...queensland/story-e6frfk...
5 Jun 2010 – **Strange light** in southeast **Queensland sky**. ARTIST'S IMPRESSION: A reader from Brisbane's northwestern suburbs - who is also a forensic ...

'Strange lights' draw out UFO spotters
www.brisbanetimes.com.au/queensland/strange-lights-draw-out-ufo-s...
5 Jun 2010 – **Strange lights** have been spotted in the **sky** in NSW, the ACT and **Queensland**, prompting multiple UFO sightings up and down the east coast. ...

Queensland Ufo's
www.mysteriousaustralia.com/strangephenomenons.html
The **lights** stayed around in the **sky** until about 6am when they finally disappeared. **Queensland** Investigations. **Queensland** seems singled out from al the vast ...
You visited this page on 12/8/11.

Strange Light in South East Queensland Sky tonight
www.godlikeproductions.com/forum1/message397266/pg1
11 posts - 2 authors - Last post: 8 Jun 2007
Hi there, did anyone else from SEQ Australia notice a Super Bright **Light** in the **sky** between 7pm and 8:30pm tonight AEST?

60   *Playing With Words*

Cymatic experiment - YouTube
www.youtube.com/watch?v=GtiSCBXbHAg
9 Sep 2008 - 2 min - Uploaded by Salerno1919
A simple experiment demonstrating the visualisation of **cymatics** can be done by sprinkling **sand** on a metal ...

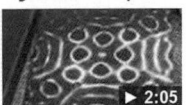

More videos for **hexagonal cymatics in sand** »

Hans Jenny -- **Cymatics** -- John Stuart Reid
www.rexresearch.com/**cymatics**/**cymatics**.htm
In this book, Chladni describes the patterns seen by placing **sand** on metal plates which .. liquid in infrasound ... life flower **hexagon cymatic** faraday chladni . ...

Cymatics
kylepounds.org/science/**cymatics**.html
Cymatics creating different shapes caused from different vibrations ... Vibration creating a column of **sand** cymatics_water_sound_image_00-500x320 ... each other Anomalies of Saturn's north pole, showing **hexagon** shape and vortex motion. ...

from Lucy Down Under | X   Inbox | X

● **LucyL Wright** to cy   show details   2 Oct (5 days ago)   ↰ Reply

Dear Jonathan,
I hope you don't mind me writing, but I've been on the internet for the last two hours searching for an explanation to something I've found, and I saw your website. Is there anything in nature that could cause cymatics to appear, say, in ordinary river sand?

Thanks for your time,
Sincerely,
Lucy Wright

↰ Reply   → Forward

☆ **Jonathan Barkley** show details 2 Oct (5 days ago) ⬅ Reply ▼

Hi Lucy,
Thanks for writing. It's pretty early hours in Scotland, but this is interesting, so though my brain's a bit fuzzy right now, here's a response, which may not be altogether what you wanted. So, Cymatics is a name we use to talk about the series of geometric forms that result when salt is say, sprinkled on a copper plate and exposed to sound vibrations. Each note actually has its own frequency that results in different geometric forms. Galileo was probably the first guy to write about it in 1632, and in 1680 Robert Hook ran a violin bow across the edge of a glass plate which he'd covered with flour, and saw amazing geometric patterns. By 1787 Ernst Chladni brought these findings into the public eye, so sometimes the shapes are called 'Chladni Patterns'. "Cymatics" is from the Greek TA KYMATIKA, which means something like, "matters pertaining to waves."

Now, as far as these patterns go in nature, I have very little insight on that. I'm a music student in my first year at university, and am just playing around with these patterns for fun. I run workshops for school kids in my spare time and am constantly fascinated by the visuals we can get from sound vibrations.

As far as shapes appearing in river sand, well, my guess is that the only force in nature able to cause that would be a human force--albeit a very artistic one. You'll have to tell me more.

Oh, there is one thing in nature that is causing something like cymatics, but it has even scientists befuddled. Have you seen the hexagonal storm on Saturn's north pole? NASA has great pics. Cause is unknown.

Best wishes,

Jonathan
- Show quoted text -

(Davidow, 2013: 11–12)

> **ABSENT NARRATOR EXERCISE**
>
> Give any of these a try and see what happens:
>
> - *Monologic narrative*: Write an extract of about 300 words, using diary entries. Perhaps the narrator will confess a secret!
>
> - *Dialogic narrative*: Write a 300-word extract made up of a letter, email or text message exchange. Allow the messages to reveal the nature of the relationship between the sender and the receiver.
>
> - *Polylogic narrative*: Create a 300-word narrative by mixing diary entries or letters with newspaper or TV reports.

This device works just as well in non-fiction and poetry. A series of newspaper clippings, letters or diary entries can tell a story without any ostensible narrator. But of course the narrator is still directing, writing and creating. We just don't feel her presence, and the resulting 'voice' is a subtle one, relying heavily on all the voices in the narrative for its quality.

Let Me Tell You Something: The Intrusive Narrator

If the absent narrator is an invisible presence, then the intrusive narrator is a visceral presence. Many well-loved children's books have unnamed but intrusive narrators who barge into the narrative, give moral lessons and tell the reader who's nice, who's horrible and exactly what you should think. C. S. Lewis does this; Roald Dahl does too, and so does Enid Blyton. Moral judgements include statements like 'He was a such a bad parent!' or 'This next part you will find frightening.' Or 'Enough of that!' and 'What a good little boy he was!'

Although this may work for those books, it can be unsettling to have a story constantly filtered through the narrator's lens. The voice is obvious. As readers of a story with an intrusive narrator, we become much more closely aligned with the listener of old, just as the narrator becomes a storyteller persona. But there are degrees of intrusiveness, as there are degrees of narrator involvement. Some of the qualities of an intrusive narrator can be harnessed for sophisticated literary leaps in creating innovative adult fiction or non-fiction. Those leaps take us to the intrusive voice found in metafiction.

Metafiction

Meta- means 'self-referential'. So metafiction is fiction or any creative narrative that is aware of itself. In metafiction the narrator purposefully exposes how the narrative is constructed. At its worst, metafiction can be the ultimate navel gaze. At its best, it comes close to illuminating the narrative in its barest truth, engaging the reader in considering the mechanics, the craft and thoughts behind the narrative. Here is an extract from Paul's memoir *Soldier Blue*:

> So here I am, back on the banks of Lake Kariba, staring out at the dead water, listening to the roar of another plane I missed. If this were a novel, there would be a crescendo of action, the crunch point where the protagonist's ultimate resolve is tested and he wins. Then would come the swift denouement to the satisfying ending, where all antagonists are vanquished. If it were a movie, it would follow Vreitag's triangle, or the steps of Joseph Campbell's *Hero with a Thousand Faces*. If it were an autobiography, there would at least be some moral lesson to be learned from the struggle and triumph or defeat of the hero. But it is none of these.
>
> So herewith the anticlimax: I am assigned to spend six months as a nondescript medic to the chaplains at KGVI barracks. I am issued a weapon but no rounds. I spend my time dispensing flu medicine to HQ soldiers and injecting propen into the buttocks of RAR soldiers. (Williams, 2008: 412)

> **INTRUSIVELY METACOGNITIVE METAFICTIONAL NARRATIVE EXERCISE**
>
> Write a piece (250–300 words) in which you, the narrator, intrude into the narrative and refer to its structure, its theme or your choice of form. Draw attention to the making of the story.

Irony

Irony happens in the gap between what the reader knows and what the narrator says. The measure can also be the discrepancy between what is said and what is meant. A character may say one thing, but we are intended to think another. Irony can be conveyed verbally or dramatically. An ironic voice is often very compelling. Here's an example from a short story by Paul:

'You remember how I dumped you for that marine?'

She actually is saying it. Actually admitting that she took a sledgehammer to my heart. And every word of hers is another wham of that sledgehammer. Even now.

'I'm very happy for you.' Smiley face.

An irony icon would be good. Irony is the distance I have travelled away from her. The brick wall I have managed to construct to keep her out. And she can feel it, I am sure. Or maybe not. She keeps babbling as if she has just found a long-lost buddy.

'You remember Travis, don't you? A marine on tour in the Middle East. We got married and we had a beautiful baby together, who is now seven.'

Brick wall icon. 'Why do I want to know all this? Why are you telling me all this? I don't want to know about beautiful babies and marines and tours and how happy you were to leave me.'

'Hear me out, please Bryan. There is a point to all this.'

'Not a sharp point, I hope.' Irony icon.

'Well, there is. He turned out to be a real prick. Asshole. Bastard.'

'I could have told you that before you twisted my heart into a piece of mangled nuclear waste that no one would go near for ten years.'

'I dumped him. My husband. Took my baby and we walked out. After I smashed the happy family photo on his head.'

'A lot of dumping going on here, Angie. You're a serial dumper, you know that? You dumped your first boyfriend for me. You dumped me for Travis. Now you dump him. Dump, dump, dump.'

'Do I detect a little bitterness here?'

'Bitterness? From someone who ruined my life? Naah. And you're still not getting any of my irony.'

SHELLEY

If there were ever selection criteria for 'what makes a great friend' then the ability to get and use irony would have to be one of them. I love irony because without it, life and everything would be so dull. There's double irony in the above extract, and maybe that's what makes it so enjoyable to read.

> **TRICKY IRONY EXERCISE**
>
> Write a passage (150 words) in which there is a discrepancy between the narrator's words and the obvious reality of a situation. The piece could be non-fiction or fiction.

A Myriad of Impressions: First-person Stream of Consciousness

We don't think in sentences with commas and full stops and semicolons. Our thoughts are much more random. Virginia Woolf's novels attempted to imitate the way impressions and images flitted through our minds. It is a good exercise to stop and examine these thoughts:

> Examine for a moment an ordinary mind on an ordinary day. The mind receives a myriad of impressions – trivial, fantastic, evanescent or engraved with the sharpness of steel. From all sides they come, an incessant shower of innumerable atoms; and as they fall, as they shape themselves into the life of Monday or Tuesday, the accent falls differently from of old. (Woolf in McKeon, 2000: 741)

Early Buddhist scriptures referred to 'stream of consciousness' as a theory of mind. But it was nineteenth-century American psychologist, William James, whose labelling of the 'stream of consciousness' became the catchphrase that took hold.

> Consciousness, then, does not appear to itself chopped up in bits. Such words as 'chain' or 'train' do not describe it fitly as it presents itself in the first instance. It is nothing jointed; it flows. A 'river' or a 'stream' are [sic] the metaphors by which it is most naturally described. In talking of it hereafter let us call it the stream of thought, of consciousness, or of subjective life. (James, 1890: 239)

Modernist writers James Joyce, Virginia Woolf and William Faulkner experimented with stream of consciousness as a new and exciting narrative technique to create unique voices. The aim was to provide a textual equivalent to our wild, wide stream-of-thought processes.

For example:

> Suddenly I'm falling tumbling into a bottomless vortex explosions of colour memories of the past dreams of the future and the old watertank is rough against my back and his laughter is louder than usual school will be out soon little boys in uniforms running all over the forest, yes even to the watertank and I wonder at the smell of jasmine and the old people we will become if he only leans a bit closer and his parents are Catholic and my Jewishness is a line that divides if only I were blonde like the girl he loved I am not the first one to want to leave Africa for America and have first world dreams I am trapped in dull clothes and the clumsy movements of a teenage self.

Narrative of course, is a proxy. Is this how we tell stories? Yes. Is this how we think? No. We think at lightning speed and in complex images. What we acquire through stream of consciousness writing is an approximation of our thought processes and the associative narrative of our minds, which jumps from one image or thought to another, stimulated by sense impressions, memories and millions of other thoughts.

Descartes, the seventeenth-century French philosopher and mathematician, believed that we *are* our thoughts. We are continually thinking, even when asleep, and this thinking or dreaming stream he identified as the 'self'. You can live without a body, he said (yet to be established by modern scientists and philosophers), but not without thoughts. *Cogito ergo sum*: 'I think therefore I am' means that I *am* my thinking self.

> **I THINK, THEREFORE I AM: STREAM-OF-CONSCIOUSNESS EXERCISE**
>
> For three minutes, write down exactly what you are thinking. Try to record every thought that comes to mind, without stopping or punctuating or pausing to reflect.
>
> Is this exercise technically impossible? Yes, because we think faster than we write and our words are just a proxy for our thoughts. But to try to get at an approximation of who you are (if you are your thoughts, that is, as Descartes believed), then let's try to record the thinking self. At the very least, this exercise allows us to observe our associative, meandering thought patterns (similar to the word-association exercise) as we write.

The technique gives the reader an insight into the workings of a character's mind in a way that omniscient or first-person narration cannot. We are not telling a story here, or portraying voice: we are *showing voice in action*.

The world we navigate every day is swimming in a sea of brilliant narratives. And as well-loved Victorian author George Eliot says, there exist many 'good' ways to tell them. As long as readers enjoy the narrative, Eliot says, 'Why should a story not be told in the most irregular fashion that an author's idiosyncrasy may prompt …?' (Eliot, 1884: 287).

Past or Present Tense

The choice to write in either the present or past tense is also a consideration of voice. It is an issue of where we want the reader to stand while we tell our story. What point of view – past or present or future? We could tell our saga in retrospect, looking back at events that happened in the past. Or we could bring our readers along with us and let the story unfold 'before our very eyes' in the present. Or we could set our story in the future, about events that have not yet occurred.

SHELLEY
The choice of which tense to use is usually intuitive to me and has a lot to do with the 'voice' of the piece. Each of my narratives tends to dictate which tense will work best. Sometimes I've had to go through and change everything, but most of the time, by the first sentence I've already located my reader and narrator in time.

Past tense is what you would expect in a story. The narrator sits in the present, telling us what happened in the past. And then … and then … But people use present tense in storytelling to give immediacy to the writing, as if the action is unfolding in the moment.
Why use either? What is the difference?
Theo Damsteegt suggests that 'the present tense serves to establish a seemingly direct, unmediated link with a character's mind' (2005: 39).
Here's Addie returning from a few chapters ago, first in the past and then in the present tense.

> Addie was twenty-two, a history student at the University of Hull, fiercely independent, anti-male, anti-anything slim; pale, very English, and in love with Australia. Well, the idea of Australia. All her friends had done the obligatory clichéd tour down under: Byron Bay, the Rocks, Uluru, Great Barrier Reef. No, not that Australia. She wanted to get under the glossy skin of the country. To throw herself into something unusual.
>
> Addie is twenty-two, a history student at the University of Hull, fiercely independent, anti-male, anti-anything slim; pale, very English, and in love with Australia. Well, the idea of Australia. All her friends have done the obligatory clichéd tour down under: Byron Bay, the Rocks, Uluru, Great Barrier Reef. No, not that Australia. She wants to get under the glossy skin of the country. To throw herself into something unusual.

The second example is much more immediate, closer to us, and we are seeing her enacting her desires in front of our eyes.

But which is better for the story?

The first implies that the narrator knows the ending, that we are looking back at the story, reflecting. The second implies that the narrator and reader are in it together, experiencing the action simultaneously. The French literary theorist Roland Barthes called this 'writing degree zero', with no reflective distance between past and present. For Barthes, writing should be an eternally intransitive 'here and now' utterance. By paring back the words from their author's biological and historical context (Barthes in the 1960s declared the author to be dead, just as Nietzsche had declared in the previous century that the omniscient God was dead), now all that is left are 'words, vertical and vertiginous, that jut like monoliths ... into a totality of meanings, reflexes and recollections' (Barthes 1967: 47). The word is reduced to zero degree.

What does this mean for writers? That we can pare down meanings and context and authorial intrusion, and allow the words to exist as themselves. An example? Barthes admired Albert Camus's *The Stranger*, and this novel is worth reading to see how the author pared out emotional and historical baggage from his writing and wrote in the 'focalized' present tense.

Here is an example in the style of Camus:

> She raises her hand. Her fingers are inky. She fiddles with a pen. She tosses her red hair away from her face. 'Are there rules about what we should write?' she asks.
>
> The others are engrossed in their own narcissism now, deep into threads of narrative, crouching over laptops, iPads, thumbing phones, or scratching on pieces of paper. She has written nothing.
>
> He stands by her desk and gives her the platitude he is going to regret for the whole semester. 'This is creative writing: you can write about anything you like.'
>
> She gives him a quick stab of a glance and he sees, for an instant, black eyes.
>
> 'Your name?'
>
> 'Phoebe French.'
>
> Fingernails chewed down to the cuticles, swollen fingers, heavy boots and thick socks, creased T-shirt, a mass of dark red hair that covers her face. She jabs a furtive look at her neighbour, who is engrossed in her freewriting, and addresses her fingers.

WRITING DEGREE ZERO – OR NOT – EXERCISE

Write a passage (200 words) in the past tense. Rewrite the same passage in the present tense, and enjoy taking note of the subtle shifts that impact how the narrative moves.

PAUL

In the countless writing workshops in which I participated in universities in the United States, I remarked how most of the stories presented were in the present tense. The majority of them were crisply crafted, and the present tense was used without question. Once I asked a student why she was using the present and not the past tense, and she said, 'Am I? I didn't realize'. In other words, she was not consciously making a choice, or writing degree zero for a purpose, but as following a trend. I found stories in the present tense to be better crafted but also dry and skeletal, and soulless. It is easier to remove emotion and messy nostalgia while writing present tense. And sometimes it is a good way to clean up messy writing.

I have tried telling a story in future tense. But it cannot work for too long because it feels speculative:

> Tomorrow he will go to see her. He will tell her what he really thinks, that he has been in love with her forever, and she will embrace him and say, 'I can't believe you waited so long to tell me this – I have also been in love with you.' And they will live happily ever after.

Some new writers bop around uncontrollably between past and present tense. The following exercise should serve as a prophylactic and also cure most tense issues if they are happening at present.

In this short piece, the first paragraph is in the present tense. The second is in the past tense and talks about what happened yesterday. The third paragraph is in the past perfect and refers to an incident way back in the past. The last paragraph comes back to the present.

> From my window I watch the activity on the street below. A boy catches my eye. He is cycling dead straight in the middle of the road, hands free, his hair blown back by the wind, his smile visible even from here.

Yesterday, he did the same thing. But he had to use one hand on the handlebars to steady himself, and the bike went all over the road. When the wheel went out from under him, and bike and boy crashed into the pavement, raucous laughter from just out of sight ensued.

It reminded me of my first bike. I'd got it as a present when I was ten. I had been freewheeling down a hill when the wheel twisted, and I was catapulted head-over-heels over the handlebars. Pride comes before a fall, my father had said while I was having stitches.

I still have the scar on my chin. As the boy makes it to the end of the road with his hands held high, wild applause greets him from the group of kids standing on the curb.

KEEPING THINGS IN TENSE EXERCISE

Write a piece (300–500 words) in which the narrative follows the tense structure set out in the example.

- Write paragraph 1 in the present tense, and locate the narrator here and now.
- Write paragraph 2 in the simple past tense, referring to something that happened yesterday.
- Write paragraph 3 about a memory from long ago, in the past perfect tense.
- Write the final paragraph back in the present tense, where the narrator is currently located.

RESOURCES TO HELP YOU KEEP PERSPECTIVE AND NOT LOSE YOUR VOICE

For various points of view, read *Huckleberry Finn* (unreliable first-person narrator), *The Great Gatsby* (outside narrator), Ernest Hemingway's 'Hills Like White Elephants' (detached third-person objective), Calvino's *If on a Winter's Night a Traveler* (second person), George Eliot's *Middlemarch* or Jane Austen's *Pride and Prejudice* (omniscient).

Robert Browning's 'Porphyria's Lover' is an example of narrative poetry with an unreliable narrator.

For examples of epistolary writing, Stephen King's *Carrie* is a multi-media novel, and Alice Walker's *The Color Purple* is a correspondence between two characters, as is *The Bridges of Madison County*. *Bridget Jones's Diary* is a journal, or diary.

For metafiction, read John Barthes's *Lost in the Funhouse*.

The classic stream of consciousness writers were James Joyce (read *Portrait of an Artist as a Young Man*), Virginia Woolf (*Mrs Dalloway* or *To the Lighthouse*), and William Faulkner (*Sound and the Fury* or *As I Lay Dying*).

5
Really Bad Writing: Melodrama, Sentimentality, Overwriting and Lazy Writing

> **Freewrite # 5**
>
> *He gazed longingly at her retreating figure ...*

There is an empire built on the overuse and abuse of adjectives. 'Descriptive words' are the lifeblood of school English classes. It's a safe assumption that from the time we first start writing our own creative stuff, we are encouraged by our teachers and parents (well-meaning editors that they are) to make our work 'colourful', to add a plethora of rich, perfumed and full-fat adjectives that apparently enhance our poetry and prose. The empire extends further and includes vampires who burn the pages of young adult fiction and who catch innocent and unsuspecting readers in their nets of repressed and unresolved sexuality. Romance and horror can easily be fed by the juicy overuse of adjectives, and with regular frequency some 700-page book, saturated with melodrama and mindlessly overwritten, makes it onto the bestseller list.

But those books do not pass the time test. They vanish quickly into oblivion. Granted, some writers who barely glance down at the words they write may end up making a fortune, and some who craft their work to death may never get published, but in the end, in the long-lasting classics, in the poetry left behind that has changed people's lives, there is always evidence of astute, sometimes breathtaking wordcraft. And of course anyone reading this book would probably be interested in creating prose and poetry that will have lasting value.

Melodramatically Sentimental Overwriting

When the word *melodramatic* is used, we usually mean it negatively. 'She's so melodramatic!' But Steven Spielberg unashamedly admits that in his motion pictures

> everything is melodrama. I don't think I've ever not made a melodrama. *E.T.* is melodramatic, and so is *The Sugarland Express*. I mean, there's melodrama in life and I love it. It's heightened drama, taking things to histrionic extremes and squeezing out the tears a bit. (Spielberg in Cherry, 2005: 1)

Let's love the melodramatic – at least for a bit and because it's fun. We have all, at one time or another (even if we were only twelve at the time), been held captive by its power. We've detested the melodramatic villain in a narrative; we've cheered for the hero; we've feared for the damsel in distress and adored the comic hero. And we've cried at the end of melodramatic books and films.

Life, lived fully, can be dramatic. How we choose to convey that drama, whether we're writing a non-fiction account of a refugee's struggle to escape a violent homeland, creating a poem about the loss of a beloved person or writing a thriller in which the planet's very existence is in question, is always our choice.

And some choose melodrama.

In melodrama everything is exaggerated, overstated. When we write it, we intensify sentiment, exaggerate emotions and relate sensational and adjectivally laden thrilling action with stock characters whom we can easily identify with.

Movies do this every day and make us cry and then feel good afterwards. Thriller writers do it, romance writers do it, horror writers do it and some do it very badly indeed!

But as writers who read, we know that melodrama is a quick bypass of real empathy. It uses gimmicks to manipulate its readership. The words, clichéd events and stock characters are triggers for our most basic emotional reactions, and so readers aren't given the opportunity to develop empathy, to change the way they see things because they've been truly moved. Melodrama is like refined sugar. We crave it, devour it, but it offers little nourishment and eventually, after too much (which is relative, of course), we might even feel sick.

Even so, melodrama has and always will suck us into its vortex. So let's dive into it and explore what makes writing good or bad or powerful or manipulative. Early Gothic novels in the early eighteenth century were overwritten melodramatic tear-jerkers (and bestsellers). Horace Walpole's *Castle of Otranto* (first published in 1764) was one of them:

> 'Oh! my Lord, my Lord!' cried she; 'we are all undone! it is come again! it is come again!'
> 'What is come again?' cried Manfred amazed.
> 'Oh! the hand! the Giant! the hand! – support me! I am terrified out of my senses,' cried Bianca. (Walpole, 1840: 125)

What makes this piece melodramatic? First, we can imagine the over-exaggerated emotional gestures of the characters: she swooning, holding her forehead; he, open armed. Secondly, the (over) use of exclamation marks, which 'shout' at the reader. Thirdly, the way we are told how she feels.

SHELLEY

By the time I was thirteen, I think I had read over a hundred category romances. I sat in a tree in Africa with a sandwich and a book, reading historical European romances in which stammering heroines were overwhelmed with emotion whenever the tall, dark Italian/Spanish hero entered the room; I fell for the alpha male American hero whose heart was cold and closed forever to love until the heroine came along and melted him. I swam in melodramatic romance set in faraway countries throughout my teens, and loved every overindulgent minute of it. I did at some point attempt to write category romances, but I had a habit of undermining the genre and falling into irony. One rejection letter said that my book lacked 'emotional intensity'. ☺ Here's a poem in tribute to all things melodramatic:

> I will never be your equal
> You are magnificent, beyond compare
> And I am nothing
> Nothing.
> Everything I have ever tried or attempted
> To do in honour of you
> Echoes emptiness
> Failure, misery and despair
> My life is bitterness and agony
> I am lost, worthless
> And best left
> On my own.

Make a list of narrative devices that create melodrama.

> **CHANNELLING THE MELODRAMATIC SENTIMENTAL VOICE EXERCISE**
>
> Write a short piece, either a poem or prose (80–100 words), and overdo the emotion. Make the piece up or use and amplify an emotional moment in your life. Be sentimental. A melodramatic voice is generous with its use of adverbs and adjectives and heart-wrenching, heartbreaking abstract nouns.

PAUL

I tend to be melodramatic when I'm writing about a character's feelings, and then have to return and cut mercilessly. Here's an example from an early draft of my memoir Soldier Blue:

> The trees echoed my feelings of despair. I was drowning in love. And she was the only one who could save me. I love you I love you, every cell in my body shouted out to her. But the cruel ring on her finger was a knife cutting through my heart. She looked hesitant. 'I'm so glad you're here. I have something to tell you.'
> 'You want to see me?' I spun dizzily, hungry for any morsel of her affection.
> 'I want your advice.' She looked even more nervous now. 'Promise you'll still be my friend?'
> 'I'll always be your friend, no matter what. You know that. Cross my heart and hope to die.'
> 'I want you to be the first to know.'
> The birds in the tree above us were squawking so loudly and she was speaking so softly that I had to incline my head towards her and lip-read. Her breath was warm on my face. I could hardly stand still, giddily swooning towards her. I wanted to hold her, touch her, kiss those sweet lips.
> 'I'm engaged.'
> I felt as if I had been sent to hell. Demons pulled me down into the depths of despair.
> 'Didn't you notice the ring?' She displayed the sparkling diamond set in the centre of blue amethysts as a sword, that same sparkling knife whose shafts of reflected light pierced me to the heart and left me bleeding and gutted on the ground.

And here is the same passage after I cut out all reference to emotion and decided instead to show *emotion through dialogue and silence (more on that later):*

> Outside, in the cool of the trees, she twirled a ring around her finger, bit her lip.
> 'I'm so glad you're here. I have something to tell you.'
> 'I'm all ears.'
> 'I want your advice.' Her left eyelid was fluttering. 'Promise you'll still be my friend?'
> 'Cross my heart and hope to die.'
> 'I also want you to be the first to know.'
> The birds in the tree above us were squawking so loudly and she was speaking so softly that I had to incline my head towards her and lip-read.
> 'I'm engaged.'
> A poem we had learned by heart in English the year before suddenly played in my head: a poem about the dead in hell listening to the smooth, silvery, sweet voice of an angel.
> 'Didn't you notice the ring?' She displayed the sparkling diamond set in the centre of blue amethysts as a sword, a knife whose shafts of reflected light glittered at me. (Williams, 2008)

> **EMOTION MINUS MELODRAMA EXERCISE**
>
> Rewrite your poem or emotionally loaded exercise – without the melodrama, eliminating references to emotion.
>
> Look at the result. Which is the more powerfully emotional piece?

Staggeringly Bad Writing

Bad writing can be found anywhere and everywhere. It's as frequent as fast-food outlets and just as attractive to customers. So why is it bad? And what's good writing anyway? Just because something is prevalent doesn't mean it's good. If we compare the nutritional values found in a burger and fries with a homemade organic lentil and vegetable soup, we could easily come to the conclusion that one of those meals eaten repeatedly over years will enhance well-being, and one won't!

SHELLEY

Writing a piece where every word conveys exactly what I mean it to convey is what matters most to me. Writing well is not about constantly censoring or criticizing my work as I write, but about editing, clarifying and creating art that matters for its own sake. I love a good story, but I want to make something that has some intrinsic artistic value of its own.

But! I love bad writing exercises. We can't really become good writers if we don't dive headfirst into some really bad writing and experience what it is. This example really has zero artistic merit:

> He leaned over her, and she saw only his shadow against the moonless night. His eyes glowed with passion. Her emotions paralysed her and she reached up to touch his rich brown hair, which made her heart race.

So, of course, his eyes can't glow with passion if all she can see is his shadow, and if she is paralysed with emotion, how would she reach up her hand? And again if the night was so dark and she could only see his shadow, she could not observe his rich brown hair. But if bestselling authors can do this, so can I.

BESTSELLER BAD WRITING EXERCISE

1. Write a short paragraph (50–100 words) as badly and incongruously as you can.
2. Then do a careful edit and make it 'good' or 'better' writing. What did you change? What effect does that have?

Writer's Elbow

Peter Elbow advocates that in order to write well, we need first to write badly: 'Getting rid of badness doesn't lead to excellence … . [W]e need to invite badness … we have little hope of producing excellent writing unless we write a great deal. Plenty will be bad' (Elbow, 1981: 19).

Elbow suggests that writer's block happens when we are trying to do two things at once – let our spontaneous and inspired writing pour out of us, and at the same time edit, censor and try to improve our writing, worried about what our readers will think.

So rather than try to write well initially, he suggests that we let it flow and allow bad writing.

There is a tradition of spontaneous writing, from Walt Whitman ('The secret of it all, is to write in the gush, the throb, the flood, of the moment – to put things down without deliberation – without worrying about their style – without waiting for a fit time or place … by writing at the instant the very heartbeat of life is caught', Whitman, 1970) to Kerouac's 'spontaneous prose' (see last chapter).

Elbow calls his technique 'expressivism':

> Schooling makes us obsessed with the 'mistakes' we make in writing. Many people constantly think about spelling and grammar as they try to write. I am always thinking about the awkwardness, wordiness, and general mushiness of my natural verbal product as I try to write down words. But it's not just 'mistakes' or 'bad writing' we edit as we write. We also edit unacceptable thoughts and feelings, as we do in speaking … . The problem is that editing goes on at the same time as producing … . The main thing about free writing is that it is non-editing. It is an exercise in bringing together the process of producing words and putting them down on the page. Practiced regularly, it undoes the ingrained habit of editing at the same time you are trying to produce. It will make writing less blocked because words will come more easily. (Elbow, 1972: 1)

Bad writing, however, is only the first stage of a long writing process. The second and vital stage is to bring in the editor/critic and sort out the scribblings.

Indulgent Overwriting

Mark Twain tells us to '[e]schew surplusage' (1895). He also advises us to look out for rogue modifiers: 'If you catch an adverb, kill it.'

PAUL

My biggest fault is that I overwrite. I over-explain. I say the same thing over and over to make sure I get the point across. So no matter how profound my insights are, or how amazing my subject matter is, the writing dulls and mars and obscures my ambitions. Overwriting is difficult to detect in your own writing and easier to see in others'. (See? I am overwriting this very paragraph!)

Overwriting is often the result of trying too hard to say something or being too tentative or insecure, so we keep adding more words in the hope that we will be understood. But overwriting is also easy to fix. Look out for

- overuse of technical, flowery or discordant words; and/or
- overuse of adjectives; and/or
- convoluted sentences which have multiple ideas running through them.

Swoon:

Sir Vincent galloped away furiously on his shadowy, thundering steed. Maria gazed after him longingly, lovingly, heartbroken, her pale, heart-shaped face riven with anguished tears that ran torrents down her flushed, flaming cheeks. Heaving, choking sobs racked her frail, trembling frame while misery-laden monstrous thunderclouds banked threateningly on the distant horizon.

Oh, horror:

The knife twisted in the mercenary's gut and he fell from his screaming mare, tumbling into the rising swirling clouds of parched and pale dust while bright red and crimson drops of life leached from him and splattered on the thankless barren earth.

And the descriptionarily saturated:

The heaving sea crashed against the creaking hull. Beyond the midnight reflections of the pale, broken moon, the single dark shadow of a human form clung desperately to a piece of broken, floating wreckage.

ELIMINATING SURPLUS EXERCISE

Choose one of the above paragraphs. Rewrite it, eliminating all the adjectives and adverbs. Decide whether the printed draft or your edited version has more power.

Many of us overwrite unconsciously. It's so easy to overwrite because adjectives and adverbs do the job of telling a reader what we want them to feel. The process of 'showing' readers an experience, of getting them to feel the power of an intended emotion, involves skill that can be learned and practised, and make us all better writers. But before we go on a metaphorical word cleanse, we are allowed to leap unfettered into the overindulgent world of purple prose and overwriting.

> **TOO MUCH OF A GOOD THING EXERCISE**
>
> Using the beginning of the freewrite for this section as a prompt, or any subject matter that is inspiring, write a piece of prose with as many adjectives and adverbs as possible. Go wildly, liberally, freely and indulgently overboard so that the piece emerges like a wedding cake with too many tiers, too much icing and way, way too much sugar!

After suffusing a page with adjectives and adverbs, most writers will be acutely aware of how this tactic lends itself to hyperbole, satire and, of course, melodrama. The next exercise is the cleanse after the descriptive word binge; it has been used by some of the most beloved writers throughout history to make their writing stronger. It is, perhaps, the most valuable clean-up tool in the writer's universe.

> **EXCISING ADVERBS AND ADJECTIVES EXERCISE**
>
> 1. Reread your 'Too-much-of-a-good-thing' exercise, and eliminate every adjective and adverb. Your piece of writing will shrink dramatically.
>
> 2. Take a piece of your own writing, something that is in process at the moment, and spend 20 minutes eliminating adjectives and adverbs. Additionally, replace some of the verbs with more evocative and specific ones that have greater 'weight' or 'value'.

It's not hard to see now how to increase the power of our words. As we eliminate superfluous descriptive words and use verbs to show the reader around, the writing becomes focused, unsentimental, even profound.

Lazy Writing

When the words are just slouching around on the page, doing very little, we call this lazy writing. It may not be overwriting, but it is just as dull:

> He walked into the room. She moved her head and saw him.

These particular verbs are lazy and overused. They're generic and lack specificity. If a verb is lazy, we usually (mistakenly) haul in some adverbs to help it do its job.

> He walked slowly, cautiously into the wide, high-ceilinged, expansive room. She moved her small head quickly and saw him instantly.

But this only makes it worse. Often it will work to replace the lazy, overused verbs with energetic ones which do the job efficiently and cleanly:

> He ambled into the palace foyer. She whirled around to face him.

Same with nouns. Adjectives prop up lazy nouns.

> The dog ran onto the beach.

When we want to be specific we often end up relying on the adjective to prop up the generic noun:

> The thin racing dog ran fast onto the sandy beach.

A specific noun works harder:

> The Greyhound streaked onto the sand.

We can't let the lazy verbs and nouns get away with it!

> **STREAKING GREYHOUND EXERCISE**
>
> Rewrite these lazy sentences:
>
> His mother spoke angrily.
> It rained.
> His eyes looked evil.
> He was going slowly insane.
> The sky was the colour of …
> The passengers got out of the train.
> He spoke softly and quietly.

Lazy Writing Protection

George Orwell, author and visionary (*1984, Animal Farm*), proposed rules that he believed would protect forever against lazy writing. 'Keep it simple', he believed. And *never*

- use a metaphor, simile or other cliché which you are used to seeing in print
- use a long word where a short one will do
- use the passive where you can use the active: prefer the concrete to the abstract
- use a foreign phrase, a scientific word or a jargon word if you can think of an everyday English equivalent.

Also:

- If it is possible to cut a word out, always cut it out.
- Use adjectives with economy.
- Break any of these rules sooner than say anything outright barbarous. (Orwell, 1946)

Clichés

A cliché is a lazy metaphor or simile. The word originates from the French photographic device, a stamp that faithfully reproduces the same print every time.

Writing clichés means we can't be bothered to make thoughts or images ourselves: we just rely on common phrases or words that have been used so much they sit permanently on the tips of our tongues.

In the examples of overwriting and lazy writing above, clichés abounded. The phrase 'like a cat stalking its prey', for example, is overused, and not a simile the writer had to sweat much to think of. A cliché is often the first phrase that comes to mind. If I say, 'like water off a ...' it is easy to complete the phrase. And if it is easy, it is probably a cliché.

WATER OFF A DUCK'S BACK EXERCISE

Identify the clichés in this passage, and then rewrite it, using *new* ways of saying the same thing. Watch how the writing becomes fresh and original.

The woman's hair was black as midnight. Her face was smooth as silk, but her fear had turned her white as a sheet, making her ruby-red lips stand out in stark contrast. Her eyes were as blue as a summer's sky, and they pleaded with him not to dash her hopes. She'd tried to play it dumb, but now he could tell she was as crafty as a fox.

Clichés occur because of a hardening of the arteries of language play. What was once fresh and arresting becomes ordinary. We are used to news reporters telling us how a bomb rocked the city, or how it rained cats and dogs.

A clichéd way of seeing the world results in a clichéd narrative. For example, we portray characters as types because we haven't really looked at that particular person. But if we feel every word we write, if we craft the right word for the right moment, it is difficult to write clichés. Our job as writers is not to reproduce the world as it is, but to dissect it and see through the clichés and myths. Take that earlier exercise we did with connotation. The first images that arise in our minds when we think of words like *cowboy, hero, prostitute*, and so on, are the clichéd ones. But if we go to genuine experience instead of received experience, we will bypass these clichés. What does a real cowboy look like? If we are writing about one, simply taking the first image off the shelves of our mind is not necessarily best practice.

J. M. Coetzee, the South African/Australian writer, once commented that his role as a writer was not to 'reinforce the myths of our time, but to dissect those myths' (1988: 3). If we want our writing to sparkle, to be real, we need to dissect, and not reinforce.

PAUL

Most of what we write comes not from personal experience, but from books, TV, movies, the Internet. Most of my students write stories about vampires and zombies and types because they are imitating what they know from the media. It's basically fan fiction. But if we try to write honestly about what we genuinely, truly see and experience, we can avoid merely imitating.

Here is a scene I wrote describing my mother meeting a Nazi soldier for the first time in World War II. At first I wrote the scene as a cliché – the evil Nazi cardboard cut-out villain, and then thought about it, and asked my mother what she really saw and felt when he appeared at her door to look for enemies hidden in her parents' basement.

> She unlatches the bolt and pulls open the door. Two men block the sunlight. She first sees the red armbands on their left sleeves. Crisply ironed shirts, trousers. She has never seen so much uniform before, such overkill, and so close up.
>
> Then she sees their eyes, grey to match their uniforms, mouths that are used to saying the letter 'k'.
>
> Her mouth opens. Not to scream but to exclaim. *Wau! Successone!*
>
> The men do not wait to be invited in. They push open the green wooden door and duck into the living room-kitchen-dining room with its uneven stone floors and its closed shutters and its fireplace and its mantelpiece with Mussolini staring into the future. *Permesso,* she says for them. *Entratta!*
>
> Her dress is suddenly dirty and her bare feet stained with purple.

DISSECTING THE MYTHS OF OUR TIME EXERCISE

Think of a clichéd character type or situation: the Nazi villain, a prostitute, a cowboy, a stepmother, a princess – or imagine a clichéd scene or event – a relationship break-up, a midlife crisis, a robbery. Dissect the underlying myths. Then write a 200-word piece describing the scene or character as honestly as you can, avoiding the inherent clichés.

Popular Writing

Often, popular ('pulp') fiction is meant to be consumed and discarded, and therefore popular fiction is often written badly, carelessly and with melodrama and other shortcuts. The same with so-called 'poetry' on greeting and birthday cards. As we have stated earlier in this chapter, it's like fast food sprinkled with MSG and laden with sugar so it tastes good. It can be packaged attractively too, but much of this type of fast food has little nourishment. 'Pulp' fiction and trite poetry on birthday cards leaves readers bored or hungry. Whereas a good meal, a good book or an incisive poem goes to our very soul, speaks to our heart, resonates with us and perhaps changes our life.

It does not have to be either/or. Our preference is for writing that is both popular and nourishing.

Other Deadeners and Killjoys of Writing Pleasure

Overused Modifiers

The lazy words *very, little, a bit, sort of, kind of, rather, quite, slightly, mostly* deaden our writing. If we're writing while awake and not asleep, we probably want to avoid them where possible. A 'very handsome man' is not as effective as 'a handsome man'. The word 'very' comes across as the writer trying too hard to convince the reader. If something is 'really, really good', it probably isn't. 'It was good', means exactly that.

Lazy Verbs

As we've shown, lazy verbs are ones we use all the time as a bad habit. Here are some: *be, feel, appear, seem, have*.

The worst culprit is the verb *to be* and all its forms – *am, are, is, was, were*, and so on. We use it far too much, and it sucks the life out of our writing.

'There was a man at the store' is a lazy sentence. It comes easily to us, but it kills the story or poem we are writing.

Same with 'It was raining.' Or 'He was happy.'

Was says nothing: it is just a verb placemat.

So what can we do to change our reliance on *to be*? If we substitute the *to be* verb with an apt and vibrant verb, our writing suddenly finds its feet again:

He propped himself up against the store window.
The rain machine-gunned into the earth.

86   *Playing With Words*

Other deadeners of writing are overused adjectives and adverbs. If we can find the exact noun or verb we want, we really shouldn't have to rely on clichéd descriptors to prop it up. The worst offenders in the Lazy Adjectives and Adverbs Department are words like *beautiful* or *nice* or *quite*.

> Dead: There were books on the desk.
> Cliché: Books littered the desk.
> Better: Books obscured the desk.

RESURRECTION EXERCISE

Below is a paragraph of lazy writing – possibly the laziest, deadest, most clichéd piece ever.

Identify the lazy writing (clichés, lazy verbs, adjectives, adverbs) and rewrite to eliminate all lazy writing:

> There was a very nice girl at the store. She appeared to be sort of interested in me, well, kind of anyway. She was quite pretty, and her eyes were nice. I felt rather cool as she looked at me. She seemed kind of sad, which made her look very beautiful. There was a noise behind me: a man coughed, I think. He appeared a little annoyed, but I kept staring lovingly, tantalizingly, sassily at her rather nice eyes, and she pretty much stared right back in the same way. I felt quite flattered until the man said, 'Hey, why are you staring at my wife?' There was an awkward silence. I was rather upset and saw her smile at me – sort of mocking me, I believe. I was pretty much fed up with the whole scene by now, so I walked out. It was a shame, really; it could have been the start of a beautiful thing between us.

PAUL

Again, how I avoid these clichés is to feel *the story, see the people, breathe passion into the description. Ironically, after I've just advised to avoid movies, the best way to avoid clichés is to visualize the story as a movie, with actions rather than words.*

It's okay to write melodrama and sentimental prose, even clichés at times, as long as we are in control of the writing. Tired and lazy writing, however, is unconscious, automatic and consequently often boring. Writing that wakes people up, makes them feel what it is like to live in a particular place or time or body, to see events from a unique angle is a gift to a reader. If we live into every movement and action we describe, our writing too will come alive.

Conclusion: There's a Troll in My Bathroom

Bad writing and lazy writing may come from not having the skills to craft our writing well, but it is also caused by not seeing, not writing in the moment, not being original. Second-hand descriptions and experiences tend to be bad and lazy. If you write about a troll in your bathroom, be sure you are not repeating an idea you have read before. 'There is a troll in my bathroom' is a lazy way of saying that we haven't visualized what it would really be like to a have a troll in our bathroom. Saying 'troll' is a cliché, asking our readers to summon up their own images of a troll. Rather, we might use the full power of our imagination to describe this creature. What would it really be like? Convince our readers, and they will go with us anywhere. Give them second-hand descriptions, and they won't.

> **FURTHER READING AND RELEVANT EXAMPLES**
>
> Read Peter Elbow's *Writing Without Teachers* or *Writing With Power* for a taste of how to write spontaneously and how to separate the creator from the critic in you. Elbow argues that bad writing is a necessary part of the process.
>
> Watch a few Hollywood melodramatic movies to see how our emotions are manipulated. Read some 'bad' 'pulp' fiction to see how it works. Then take a 'literary' work and read it to experience the contrast.
>
> George Orwell's *Animal Farm* and *1984* are concerned with how propaganda works and how words can be manipulated.
>
> J. M. Coetzee's novels 'dissect' rather then 'reinforce' the myths of our culture. Read, for example, *Waiting for the Barbarians* or *Disgrace* to see how he deconstructs issues of power and male sexuality yet keeps our attention in a riveting story. (Actually 'riveting' is a cliché – sorry.)

6
Silences and the Spaces Between

> **Freewrite #6**
> *A shadow crossed the moon ...*

We don't need much. A piece of paper and a pen or pencil for starters is everything. Words are our only essential material. We can make anything out of them, and the worlds that emerge can be all consuming to the consumers. This, of course, ensures that those of us who use them well will always have a line-up of readers waiting for the next poem, book, instalment or chapter. And as story makers of one kind or another, we may well be the only artists in the universe who do not have to spend any money at all on our materials. If we have a voice, we can tell a story. But not only that: the element that makes our written material work well is invisible, intangible and as cheap as a single sheet of paper – emptiness, space. Between words. Behind words. Between lines. Beyond narratives – space where words could be, but where they've been left out or taken out.

The 'spaces between' honour the creative power of the writer's imagination – and importantly, the reader's imagination. It's hard to imagine that a whole chapter can be written on nothingness, but here it is.

PAUL

Good writing is like circling a black hole, stitching around it and making it visible. Poetry in particular lends itself to the black hole analogy, but the same goes for fiction and non-fiction, memoir and genre fiction: the more we imply things, often the more power they have.

I am intrigued by what many writers and critics called the unnameable (Badiou), the inexpressible (Lyotard), the ineffable (Beckett), the abject

(Kristeva), the other (Derrida), the uncanny (Freud) and what lies beyond language (Wittgenstein), all ways of describing what is outside of our writing but visible through our writing.

There is, in other words, a 'secret' truth in literature.

The big question is, where does this secret reside and how do we create it – or find it? In any written work of art, realities and truths lie in the spaces between our words.

What we leave out is just as significant as what we put in.

In that intriguing space where no words exist, our imaginations get to work. Omitting things is a deliberate act by writers that credits readers with the capacity to fill in gaps in exposition. Together, we writers and readers turn areas of nothingness into story, poetry, truth, enlightenment.

Anyone who has ever tried writing a sex scene will know that even at this most obvious level, the art of omission comes in handy. A 'less is more' approach can save us. It might even elevate a scene and its characters out of Cringeville into transcendence:

> They reached for each other as the late moon set.
> The next morning, he spoke as if they were strangers.

In the gap, the reader writes the story.

There is, of course, a balance between crafted silences and gaping holes in narratives where readers get lost, and it's this balance we hope to achieve in our writing. So while we want to stitch a tight seam around an event rather than drag a reader painstakingly through every moment, we don't want to leave such big gaps between the stitches that readers will just fall though. In *About Time: Narrative, Fiction and the Philosophy of Time*, Mark Currie suggests that a 'work of literature is all on the surface, all there in the words on the page, imprinted on a surface that cannot be gone behind' (2001: 152).

And yet, that's what we do as we read and write. We always go behind. Sometimes we don't know exactly what it is that we've gone behind, but we soon find out. As creators we develop themes and subtexts. The invisible threads that pull readers through a narrative or a poem are most often implied. By the end of a powerful piece in any genre, the invisible, the intangible and the unwritten come to life as narrative.

SHELLEY

When I write, I'm aware that I am not the only creature pouring meaning into the spaces behind the words I type – I know that the minute readers come along and bring their personal universes and interpretations to the work and fill in the blanks, something gets 'unburied' from the text. And the 'thing' that gets unburied is hopefully pretty close to the 'thing' that I buried, though even if that is the case, for each person it will resonate differently and have a slightly different meaning. I love that.

Great literature is full of enigma, which is why critics and teachers often say things like 'What the author is really *trying* to say is …'. Of course, the author is *not* trying and then failing to say something because of bad communication skills. We'd be more accurate if we said, 'What the reader is really trying to uncover is …'. The critic or reader is on a metaphorical treasure hunt to discover whatever themes and messages lie buried in the writing that maybe even the writers themselves are unaware of.

Minimalism, Icebergs and Truth

Here is the shortest story possibly ever written, attributed to Ernest Hemingway, master of minimalism:

For sale: Baby shoes, never worn.

Hemingway did not write well by writing very little; he wrote well by leaving most of what he had written out. 'I write one page of masterpiece to ninety-one pages of shit,' he once confessed. 'I try to put the shit in the wastebasket.'

Another prolific writer, Truman Capote, who wrote the first Creative Non-fiction novel, *In Cold Blood*, admitted that he used only 20 per cent of the material he had initially written in his final draft. Final products are deceptive. It happens with movies, music and literature. We assume that what we see is what we get, that this is how the product was constructed. But a novel may have gone through a hundred drafts; a poem may have been scratched out a thousand times, each word rewritten; and songs we hear in the media, layered and layered and scrapped and redone. If we view directors' cuts of movies or watch the omitted or cut scenes, we begin to get a sense that the final product is the tip of a very large iceberg.

Let's take a close look at minimalist writing: in essence, the approach implies everything by action. Vocabulary is pared down, and sentence structure is basic. There's no 'fancy' footwork. Stories do not explain or resolve – they reveal. The narrator is absent, the tense present, the person an objective third or first. Dialogue drives plot and reveals character. Adjectives and adverbs are scarce.

So, if we're ever afraid we might be overwriting, minimalism can save us. Literary minimalism is all about creating content that is stripped down to what is essential in form or content or both, and allowing a reader to fill in the gaps. Our brains enjoy working hard and creating meaning, linking and inferring rather than being given everything on an explicit platter. Minimalism can give words power. Below is a 'minimalist' piece, which reveals the essential characteristics in its style.

> The teacher taps her desk with the stick.
> 'Pesce d'Aprile? Daydreaming again?'
> She opens her eyes. 'Sorry, Dottore Cisa.'
> The girls behind snigger. She hunches over her belly so that her dress billows out and nothing shows.
> 'And take that fish off her back. Do you know you have a fish glued onto your back?'
> 'Sorry, Dottore.'
> The teacher tears the paper cut-out off her dress. 'You must learn to stand up to them.'
> 'Si, Dottore.'
> 'And stop calling me "Dottore".'
> 'Si, Dottore.'

In the example above, the character hides her 'condition' by hunching over. We might infer, even in a brief example, that she's pregnant and underage, and that she's being bullied by classmates because of it. But that entire reality is under the surface, and at the tip of this proverbial iceberg is a simple description of what the character does and what the teacher says.

The iceberg analogy comes from Hemingway:

> If a writer of prose knows enough about what he is writing about he may omit things that he knows and the reader, if the writing is written truly enough, will have a feeling of those things as strongly as though the writer had stated them. The dignity of movement of an iceberg is due to only one-eighth of it being above water. (Hemingway, 1932: 192)

Hemingway was good at throwing one-liners at journalists and interviewers, and these one-liners are still used frequently in Facebook and blog postings to encourage (or discourage) writers. Here is one: *All you have to do is write one true sentence. Write the truest sentence that you know* (Hemingway, 1964). Easier said than done. But if we think about it, what is the truest sentence we have written? How can a sentence, a mere grammatical series of words, be 'true'?

If we know what we are writing about, we can write around what we know, without being explicit. Without actually mentioning it, we can create the weight of a subject that a reader can clearly identify even when it cannot be found in a single word or sentence.

So, with reference to icebergs and truth, here is an exercise:

ICEBERG AND TRUTH EXERCISE

Write a one-page piece that includes a conversation between two characters. Use skeletal dialogue, and refrain from using speech tags ('he said,' 'she said') except when absolutely necessary. There may be some big iceberg of a reality beyond the dialogue, but the characters never mention it. *Show* the truth about something, and describe only concrete circumstances of that truth.

As a follow-up, ask a reader, partner or fellow writer to respond to your piece and tell you what sensations your writing elicits.

Raymond Carver (1938–1988), who revitalized the short story in the 1980s, advocated for a minimalist approach to writing:

> It's possible, in a poem or a short story, to write about commonplace things and objects using commonplace but precise language, and to endow those things – a chair, a window curtain, a fork, a stone, a woman's earring – with immense, even startling power. (Carver, 1981)

Using an object as a starting point, and focusing on the details of that with precision and clarity, stories emerge. A narrative or poem might even find its power through such an exercise. In this subtle territory of inference, elision and ambiguity, we have the opportunity to draw readers into a universe in which they become co-creators of the reality. This works in both fiction and non-fiction, in poetry and prose:

The earring lay on his car seat, breaking the light. Opal in the triangular silver casing reflected in the midday sun ... its presence demanded attention. Sure enough, his wife picked it up between two fingers and held it at eye-level.

'It's beautiful,' she said.

'I swear I've never seen it before in my life,' he said.

> **IMBUING OBJECTS WITH POWER EXERCISE**
>
> Take an object (a fork, an earring, a stone) and place it in a story of 500 words. Describe its essential qualities without abstracting. Endow it with power and use it. Find simple, 'commonplace but precise' words, avoiding unnecessary adjectives, adverbs and metaphors.

Unleashing the Editor

Some writers have scrupulous editing habits. They may edit a story twenty or thirty times, and even again, after it is published, continue to edit it down. Well, that was what Raymond Carver did, apparently. Other writers (and just take a close look at any number of mass-produced paperbacks) may not.

SHELLEY

I tend to edit sections of my work as I go along. I feel I can't move on to chapter 2 until I feel chapter 1 is clean – not perfect, because nothing is ever perfect, but solid enough to allow me to go on to the next step. I rework and rewrite as I create so that I feel like I'm not building castles on foundations that may crumble. This makes for pretty slow going. So it's also not possible for me to ever say how many drafts I write. Each day, each time I come back from a break, I'm writing a new draft.

We can learn from Raymond Carver's meticulous editing practices. He claimed to spend all morning deliberating over whether to put a comma in a sentence, and then all afternoon deliberating whether to take it out. Why? Because '[t]hat's all we have, finally, the words, and they had better be the right ones, with the punctuation in the right places so that they can best say what they are meant to say' (Carver, 1981).

> **THESE HAD BETTER BE THE RIGHT WORDS EXERCISE**
>
> In this three-step exercise, take a longer piece you have written and cut it down to 500 words; then cut that to 100 words and finally reduce that to 50 words, without resorting to paraphrasing or telling. Just take out the first layer of non-essentials, then the second and then the third. Think of Hemingway's one-sentence story.
>
> Discuss the results and the potential value of the exercise.

Minimalist Grammar and Some Breaking of Rules (Again)

The minimalist approach to poetry and prose allows for particular word choices that create specific gaps. And one of the best ways of creating gaps is by using sentence fragments of a certain kind, which act as clues, providing poetic hints at the Stuff that Lies Behind. In chapter 2 we looked at sentence fragments and showed that there is indeed a place for the fragment, which isn't only as the victim of some teacher's or editor's furious pen. But now we're going to evolve the use of fragments to the next level. Here's an Imagist poem by Ezra Pound:

> *The apparition of these faces in the crowd:*
> *Petals, on a wet, black bough.*

This short poem is obviously a sentence fragment. But of a particular kind: it makes use of parataxis. Parataxis is 'the juxtaposition of clauses or phrases without the use of coordinating or subordinating conjunctions as in *It was cold; the snows came*' (*American Heritage Dictionary*, 4th edition). Or, 'the placing of clauses or phrases one after another without coordinating or subordinating connectives, from New Latin and Greek, "the act of placing side by side"' (*Merriam-Webster Online Dictionary*).

The very structure of a paratactical sentence creates a silence into which the reader can go and make meaning. An example of a paragraph with parataxis:

> At home, empty chairs, table set for two, frozen meal for one. Silence crept through the dark corridors; he closed off most of the house to make it smaller. At work, too much noise, emptiness of a different kind.

Parataxis can be used to represent the layers in a character's fleeting thoughts (rarely do we think in full sentences). And if that's so, then its corollary, the literary device hypotaxis, elongates sentences to allow for the writer to pile up images consecutively and build emotional potential. Hypotaxis is the opposite of parataxis in that clauses are subordinated or coordinated to one another in full sentences (connecting phrases with the words *but* or *and* or *although* or *however*, etc). But the difference between an ordinary sentence and a hypotactic one is that the subordinations and conjunctions function differently. Here is a sequence of 'normal' sentences:

> She sat as far away as possible from him that morning in school, although she could not avoid his accusing stares. Since he was never going to go away, she decided to outstare him instead. She made sure to glare at him at every opportunity. He soon regretted everything.

The connectives are logical. But in a hypotactical sentence, the connectives create another effect:

> She sat as far away as possible from him that morning in school and could not avoid his accusing stares, but he was never going to go away and she decided to outstare him instead, and she made sure to glare at him at every opportunity, and he soon regretted everything.

In this example, hypotaxis is the (conventionally seen as grammatically poor) overuse of the preposition *and*. The effect (not much encouraged by English teachers, lecturers, editors) is to make the prose expansive and declarative and spare and relentless.

So there is always a place for rule-breaking, and when used at the right place and the right time, both parataxis and hypotaxis can lend emotional weight to a subject and elevate us and move us.

PARATAXIS AND HYPOTAXIS EXERCISE

Write a 150-word paragraph using both parataxis and hypotaxis. Choose a subject matter that lends itself to a hypnotic rhythm.

Litotes

A litote is a narrative device that uses irony to create a distance between what is said and what is meant and enables readers to read beneath the surface of the words, even against the meaning of the words. It can be used for powerful effect in dialogue. For example:

> 'How are you?'
> 'Not too bad.'
> 'But how are you, really? Did it hurt?'
> 'It was only a little operation – nothing to worry about. I think they got it all. And I can almost pee normally again.'

Dispassion

If an actress in a movie bursts into floods of tears and howls with grief, viewers may just let her cry alone. But if we watch her from behind, seeing only her back from the point of view of a dispassionate camera as she struggles to contain her grief, we may all soon be crying with her. This comparison marks the difference between showing all and suggesting all. A highly charged emotional experience can be just beyond what the camera shows and affect the viewer profoundly.

Third-person narrative can be the perfect position to take if we want to apply the art of 'dispassion' and 'leaving things out' to emotion. If leaving out emotionally loaded words is the micromanagement of a piece, leaving out all reference to emotion is macro-management. And using the third-person objective narrator can be the deal-breaker when it comes to saving writing from being marred by sentimentality. When we use a third-person objective narrator who gives the reader 'the facts' in a dispassionate way, the writing will cry out for readers to feel what lies hidden as they make sense of the scene.

PAUL

I was once asked to write the story of an Iraqi refugee whose children had been killed in a car bomb in Baghdad. I could not possibly express the emotions or the grief he felt, so I simply described the actions exactly the way he told me. I left out all emotions. I used minimalism to hold back as much as possible:

> The fireball threw him back onto the pavement. He saw the car shatter and fly in pieces into the sky. He heard screaming. Maybe it was coming from his own mouth. He saw people running in the smoke, and he found himself lying on the hard concrete amidst rubble. Then he

saw that his arms were pierced with a hundred pieces of concrete and metal. His shirt was ripped. Blood seeped from what looked like a thousand knife wounds… . He ran towards the mangled wreckage of his car. He could see two bodies. They were both lying very still, one still in the frame of the wrecked car, the other on the pavement, thrown wide through the glass of the window. No more screaming, no crying. He fought his way through the flames and heat – a passer-by was trying to hold him back – and saw the blood. He went for his daughter first. She was face down, her brown hair gleaming in the sun. An arm. A leg. A head surrounded by a bloody halo. (Williams, 2012)

The Art of Omission and Stitching round Black Holes

So on several levels, we can apply our paring tools on a broad scale, one of which is to leave out the main subject and write around it in order to improve the piece. We can rely on the surrounding narrative to imply the subject and thus give it more power.

Here is a first-year creative writing student's piece where the main subject seemed too obvious. (The narrator is a teddy bear in case you're wondering!):

> One day Lola came home and sat on her bed and pulled me into her chest and lay back against her pillows with her knees pulled in tight as well. I could feel her *staccato* breath. She whispered in my ear that she was sad. Her fingers quavered and turned white as she said that a girl in her science class had told her to shut up and stop humming and that she was stupid for humming all the time and that she should be quiet and let everyone else think because she wasn't letting anyone think with all that humming and it was always so annoying. Lola squeezed my neck as thin as it would go. She did not make a sound after that. We sat with her breathing *rallentando*. I did nothing.

She followed the suggested cut: taking out the main subject (being bullied for wanting to hum all the time) so that the reader (and the teddy) would be left guessing.

> One day Lola came home and sat on her bed and pulled me into her chest and lay back against her pillows with her knees pulled in tight as well. I could feel her *staccato* breath. Her fingers quavered and turned white. Lola squeezed my neck as thin as it would go. She did not make a sound after that. We sat with her breathing *rallentando*.

98 *Playing With Words*

> **STITCHING ROUND BLACK HOLES EXERCISE**
>
> Using the freewrite from the beginning of this chapter, or a piece that you have already written, edit out the main subject. Let the readers guess. For inspiration read Hemingway's 'Hills Like White Elephants' to see the effect created when he leaves out the main subject (abortion).

From Black Holes to White Spaces

Just as the black holes we circumscribe have power, so do the white spaces themselves. These are the spaces we leave at the end of lines. They are literally there on the page, and are not just the leftovers after we've written the words. White spaces shape and focus attention; they tell readers where to look; they show progression; white spaces on a page are the literary equivalent of the three-dimensional space around objects in the world – without which we'd see nothing. The full effect of a sculpture is the result of how a solid interacts with the 'nothingness' around it. And so we can say that the full weight of a poem is felt when we look most closely at the literal white space between words, lines, stanzas. White spaces focus the reader's attention on the words, give each one power, make certain that some get extra attention. And in those spaces, poets can place the real subject of their work. The following poem reflects that to a degree. Without the title, it could take a while for the subject to emerge.

Qatari Women

Are they silhouettes
or
black holes

these stark tent shapes
against
a purple sky?

They drift
Beneath an Arabian moon.

A man approaches and

They huddle –

Present

Invisible as night.

They watch him from
The edge.

The horizon turns black, becomes

The void
Into which they vanish. (Davidow, 2005)

The subject is implied and complex. Are these women oppressed? Are they powerful observers? It is up to the reader to establish what the subject might be. White spaces are loaded with latent heat, with potential.

SHELLEY

My struggle as a writer often has to do with trying to distil a vast amount of information into words that can't contain the depth and breadth of my experiences. In the above poem, written when we lived in Qatar, I tried to encapsulate the complex experience of living in a society where women were blacked out, literally. At first, like many 'Westerners', I thought their clothing was oppressive. After living there for three years and talking to many women, I understood that being 'blacked out' was a relief to them: it gave women power to just be, to observe without being observed, without being stared at, objectified, sexualized by a male gaze. And I used white space aesthetically, literally and in the content because there are things that must exist outside, between words, beyond the text.

> **WHITE SPACE EXERCISE**
>
> Write a piece (poetry or prose of 100–200 words) that makes use of white space for effect.

Kill Your Darlings

Sometimes what we hold onto in our own writing is exactly what we need to get rid of; often a phrase, idea, sentence, paragraph or metaphor that we believe to be the heart of a piece can be in the way of a piece reaching its full potential. Sometimes we can cut out the seed of a poem or the genesis of a story, and the writing works better, becomes more itself, more powerful. Here is a 'before and after example' from *Whisperings in the Blood* (2016), Shelley's biographical memoir:

With Darlings:

Great intonation, he says. *You'll see – it'll all come back to you.*
The teacher looks at my fingers, which cling to the neck of the violin.
  Relax, he says, and his voice has the humour and kindness of many decades of teaching. *The violin's not a life raft.*
  But I fear that maybe it is. The light in his eyes is naked and raw.

Darlings Killed:

– Great intonation, he says. *You'll see – it'll all come back to you.*
He looks at my fingers, which cling to the neck of the violin.
Relax, he says. *The violin's not a life raft.*
But I fear that maybe it is.

Less and Less is More and More

Over the decades, the accepted canon in writing is that 'less is more', and there are complex reasons for this, one of which is that when readers have to work hard, when they get deeply involved in a narrative, they are invested in the text. This has far-reaching repercussions which we'll discuss later, in terms of the dissolution of the 'other' empathy. But for now, let's take the idea of 'less is more' to a fun and literal extreme. The objective in the following exercise is to write a short piece (these end up looking like narrative poems) that begins with a ten-word sentence. The next sentence has nine words, the next eight and so on, until the final sentence is a one-worder. The important thing is that the narrative builds and that each consecutive sentence says more with fewer and fewer words. Like previous exercises, this one challenges us to live the experience of building a pyramid of images that get more impressive as our materials diminish.

TEN-SENTENCE EXERCISE

Write a narrative (poem) with *only* ten sentences. The first sentence should be ten words long, the next nine and so on, until the final sentence is just a single word.

Example: *neighbour*

I cannot break my next-door neighbour's deafening power tools.
He starts them up at dawn, midday and dusk.
I hear the chainsaw tearing through sheet metal.
He shreds the waiting air for hours.
In dreams I bomb his shed.
I vaporize hacksaws and drills.
I watch dust rise.
Fool – begins again.
He screams.
No!

About the Fine Art of Elimination

The art of elimination is a powerful tool as long as we don't get scissor-happy. Being sparing can strengthen every element of our creations: plot, themes, character, dialogue.

For many writers at the beginning of a writing journey, much of what we do is unconscious. We can see that if we fill our poetry and prose with rich adverbs and adjectives and rely on them too much, we may be continuing on a trajectory to sentimentality, overwriting and prose that may range from light to deep purple.

At this point in this book's narrative, it seems appropriate to offer writers an opportunity to use some of the muscles developed through the preceding chapters and exercises. So, write a whole story, something that could even be submitted somewhere for publication!

> **FINALLY, A WHOLE SHORT-STORY EXERCISE**
>
> Now that you're well versed in the art of minimalist writing, include several aspects of minimalism from the list below, and write a new story. Try using these:
>
> 1. Characters whose internal thoughts do not appear in the text
>
> 2. Pared-down vocabulary
>
> 3. Narratives that reveal rather than resolve

> 4. The illusion of an absent narrator
> 5. Reliance on dialogue to reveal character and drive plot
> 6. Absence of non-essential adjectives and adverbs
> 7. Showing events, not telling them

Maximalism

Before anyone fears that we may be evangelical minimalists, please feel assured that even though we know that the art of leaving things out is such an important skill, the world would be a boring place indeed if no one ever wrote outside the 'less-is-more' paradigm. That rule is just made up anyway. Its function is to contain lazy, messy, self-indulgent, purple, over-the-top, indistinct voices so that they don't get to make too much noise. But the Writer's Police don't have any power over those who decry the loss of exuberant prose. There is a place for true, well-crafted flamboyance, and it seems fitting to give that kind of writing some space here. (To make up for it, we will have to leave a completely blank page afterwards.)

So, critics of minimalism say that this style of sparse limited prose focuses on the mundane and mediocre and that 'its pared down and … inexplicit aesthetic necessarily inculcates an … impoverished and ultimately valueless effect upon its reader' (Greany, 2012). Madison Smartt Bell, for example, disputes the idea of 'less is more' and suggests quite adamantly that 'less is less' (1986). John Aldridge labels minimalism 'assembly-line' fiction, and calls it 'unoriginal, homogenised and ultimately of little value' (1992). Minimalism, by privileging form over content, becomes empty, 'banal, trivial and inconsequential.'

Okay, there is something of value there. To that end, here is an example of 'Maximalism', a piece by Robyn Archbold, student at the University of the Sunshine Coast, a self-proclaimed 'Maximalist'.

> I hate minimalism. Less is less as we maximalists say. Shakespeare claimed: 'brevity is the soul of wit.' Ha! Tell that to Henry James. Tell that to JRR Tolkien. Dorothy Parker said: 'brevity is the soul of lingerie.' That should make sense to anybody, regardless of isms.
>
> I refuse to be one of the harlot harlequin herd slavering at the postmodern minimalist altar in their uniquely individual

homogeneity – all those earnest young writerly types skittering about to produce angsty artfully-wrought deep and meaningful incisively penetrating socially politically and ideologically challenging but sensitive and insightful and somewhat controversial and deeply profound of course literary melodrama in palely loitering skeletal prose that you wouldn't consider jumping into bed with under any circumstances if it was human despite your rampaging literary libido … (Archbold, 2012)

And yet … and yet … despite the criticism levelled at it, employing the idea that 'less is more' can honestly, truly, unequivocally save us when we feel overexposed; when we want our work to shine; when we look at a page of prose and feel it to be muddy, not as sharp as we want it to be; when we want a magnetic hold over our readers that drags them in, makes them identify with our protagonists, narrators, voices … makes them feel, despite their potential resistance, what we want them to feel, think what we want them to think. Makes them, to all intents and purposes, captives in the realm of the unspoken, unwritten subliminal subtext.

FURTHER READING

- For strong minimalist prose read Ernest Hemingway (1899/1961), particularly the obtuse 'Hills Like White Elephants' (1927), where the main subject of the piece is absent and the reader has to eavesdrop to guess what is going on (plot spoiler – it is an abortion, but it is never mentioned in the text). See also Raymond Carver, 'Are You A Doctor?', in *Will You Please Be Quiet, Please* (New York: Vintage, 1991).
- Annie Dillard, *The Maytrees* (Toronto: Harper Perennial, 2008).
- Ernest Hemingway, *The Old Man and the Sea* (London: Vintage, 2005).
- Cormac McCarthy, *The Road* (London: Picador, 2006).

7
Painting the Picture: Images that Light up the Sensory Cortex

> **Freewrite #7**
>
> *In the dark, he slid his leathery hands over the cave wall ...*

Our brains love unique metaphors. In a paper published in *Brain & Language*, researchers from Emory University demonstrated through the use of functional magnetic resonance imaging (fMRI) that metaphors involving texture activate the sensory cortex of a reader's brain (Paul, 2002). The research shows that if we read a sentence like 'The singer had a velvet voice' or 'He had leathery hands,' our sensory cortex lights up. But if we read, 'He had strong hands,' no sensory activity is detected. 'Strong' must be an overused adjective that evidently does not wow the brain in any way. Language that is suffused with compelling details, with allusion and metaphor allows the brain to create representations that engage the same regions that would be active if the scenes were taking place in the reality of the reader.

Picture making is the writer's world as much as it is the visual artist's or the film-maker's. We are in the business of creating territories every time we write: whether we're constructing a setting against which characters and plot unfold, or mapping the inner realms of a character's mind, we are making pictures. All narratives happen 'somewhere'. Even non-fiction narratives are built up using pictures, analogies and symbols that help connect and locate readers. And when we use metaphor and sensory images in a powerful way, when we hone our craft, we can inspire our readers' brains (and probably our own) to glow with engagement.

Dreams: Literal and Figurative Imagery

I had to get home urgently. But I found my way blocked at every turn. Cleaners rolled out hoses on the path. Crowds of refugees shuffled across in front of me. I finally got to my car in the darkness, but the headlights would not work. I drove off anyway, narrowly missing cars to the left of me. Suddenly I was aware of my father in the passenger seat. 'Go this way,' he directed. Miraculously, I made it past the traffic, driving blind.

'But you're dead. You've been dead for seven years.'

'Don't tell your mother,' he said.

In a moment, I found myself sitting on the beach. A young girl opposite me was split open from neck to groin, so I could see all her internal organs. I could not bear to look.

'She really should cover up,' said my father.

PAUL

That was last night's dream before I began to write this chapter. I have no idea what it means, but the images are vivid, visceral and emotionally charged. They are symbols of something deep in my unconscious that my conscious mind does not understand. I can try to interpret: I am collaborating on a novel with a Middle Eastern woman at the moment, and she is explaining the reason women cover their faces and hair in her country and issues of perceived nakedness in differing cultures. I am also aware in my writing that a lot of what my father said to me while he was alive guides my thinking. And I have just read a passage in a book on writing where the author compares writing a novel by intuition and without planning it out to driving in the dark with headlights on. (You can only see a few metres in front of you, but you can do the whole journey that way.)

And that's just it: dreams speak to us in the language of the unconscious. I am fascinated by the way my brain uses what we have commonly come to call literary narrative techniques in order to create bizarre narratives every night.

The language of dreams is the same language we use when we read and write poetry and fiction: figurative language. We create symbol, metaphor, analogy, metonymy and word play (puns, palindromes, acrostics) every night in our brains as a way to make sense of the world, as a way to process trauma and desire. Storytelling is innate to our humanity, and imagery affects our brains, our hearts. It takes us beyond words into the territory of soul.

> **THE LANGUAGE OF DREAMS EXERCISE**
>
> Write a paragraph (100–200 words) recounting a dream with bizarre imagery. Try to find the right words to convey the images so that a reader can get close to your experience.

Literally Impossible: Literal and Figurative Language

Literal language is commonly defined as a one-to-one correspondence of words to reality. For example, when we say, 'Jed was a bigot,' we believe the words represent exactly, literally what we mean: Jed was, indeed, a bigot.

We assume that figurative language requires a leap into the realm of comparison and metaphor. For example, everyone knows what we mean when we say, 'Jed was a toad.' Unless we're writing a fairy tale, our readers wouldn't ever think that Jed was literally a slimy amphibian. We're likening him to a toad or likening some characteristics (perhaps his looks) to those of a toad.

But if we take a closer look, there is really little distinction between the idea of 'literal' language and 'figurative' language. We go about our daily lives believing that words mean things. They don't. Not really. Words are just arbitrary marks on paper (or sounds we make with our mouths and vocal chords). Words can only ever *approximate* certain things or experiences or abstractions. Quite literally.

So (and this requires a bit of a hard think), what we call 'literal' language is itself an act of displacement, just as metaphorical language is. We replace a thing with a word so that people will know what we are referring to. A word does *not* signify its reference. That is why we have dictionaries, so we can endlessly refer to other words in order to approximate and represent things. If we do not know what a word means or refers to, the dictionary will offer us another word that approximates it (a synonym), and if we look up that word, it may give us yet another word or present us with the first word again in an absurd circularity of meaning transference. In other words, we never get to the *thing* itself either through reading or through looking up the meanings of words. We are ushered into a self-referential system of language we have invented.

This is significant because it reinforces our position as wordsmiths, as people who can only ever play with approximations of events and experiences. Somehow, though, that's where all the fun is: as writers we wrestle to make our words adequately describe events, experiences, things, people – to find words that work. They're slippery things, words. Sometimes a single adjective doesn't do the job, so we add more to make things clearer; sometimes we write ourselves into a purple corner in that respect, but any writer who has tried to accurately convey exact feelings, experiences, ideas – even physical descriptions of people, places and things – soon realizes that words are *all* figurative, all substitutes.

Literal and Figurative Language

Literal language strives to describe the world as it is, where each word means exactly what it says. When, for example, we say, 'He fell off his chair, he was laughing so much,' we mean exactly that. But sometimes words are inadequate in expressing what we are trying to say, and we have to resort to figurative language to describe the experience. We create pictures in the minds of our readers so they can see, smell, touch, taste, feel the experience.

Central to the act of writing is our constant grappling to find *'le mot juste'*. So often we need to use comparison, to make an approximation or word coins, to substitute meaning for words. And that's why images are so central, so essential. They allow us to explain or compare. They point towards meaning.

We use numerous narrative devices to represent reality, to tell our stories. In each of these literary devices, words displace other words or real things, or they employ other images to help us understand what we are trying to communicate.

Simile, Metaphor and the Cerebral Cortex

From the brain research spearheaded by neuroscientists who also happened to be novelists (Paul, 2012), we know that the impact of a well-crafted simile or metaphor makes certain neurons fire together in specific areas of the brain. When we read about hands like leather and the sensory cortex lights up, the word *leather* is suddenly associated with 'hands' and a powerful image emerges. Then follows a cascade of associative emotions and thoughts, all of which would be unique to each reader; for some readers the image may conjure up memories of a beloved dad, uncle or friend who worked hard with his hands all his life. Words become images that then defy words.

So, similes and metaphors evoke responses that go deep into the realms of sensations, moods and emotions.

And the difference between them is more than just an optional 'like'.

'He looked like a toad' is a simile, whereas 'He was a toad' is a metaphor. The simile is a simple comparison, which is logically and literally true. It's obvious that someone can look *like* a toad (heavy jowls, greenish in hue, squat and having excess blubber), but he cannot literally be a cold-blooded amphibian, which is what a literal reading would suggest. The metaphor equates two disparate images (person and toad) and smashes them together in our minds. Metaphors do much more than just compare. They connect two unfamiliar images in our brain and speak the language of the unconscious, which resonates powerfully within our cerebral cortex.

Here's an example of disparate images being used for effect from Shelley's memoir *Whisperings in the Blood*.

> Perhaps it is written in his blood: a special code which will emerge later in someone else, generations into the future, in nightmares and fears; in someone's inability to breathe. In Vilnius, the frowning buildings as he arrives stop him from breathing. (Davidow, 2016: 3)

So there's some smashing together of images: hereditary dispositions are the 'code' written in the character's blood, and the frowning buildings make the city hostile and unwelcoming. The metaphor invites the reader to feel what the character might be feeling.

From the Analogous to the Allegorical – Expanding the Figurative

Analogy and allegory are logical comparisons or explanations. If our readers are on one side of the bridge, we usher them to the other through use of analogies and allegories. Or, to use another analogy, we tell two stories, one on the surface and one hidden. An analogy expands a simile or metaphor; an allegory uses the surface story to explain a deeper one:

> The tyrant controlled her domain without restraint.
> If you sat on the wrong chair – beware
> Tantrum
> An hour's worth of deafening
> Torture

Or
Perhaps breakfast was not
To her liking
Not served fast enough
Screams
Punishment
Her subjects scuttled in fear
Holding their ears
Trying to appease
Their two-year-old tyrant –
Moving tentatively around
The house they once ruled.

This poem alludes, at first glance, to the suffering of people under some kind of dictatorship. By the end it is clear that the poem is an analogy: the dictator is a two-year-old child – the subjects, the ineffectual parents.

> **TOAD ON A FIRST DATE EXERCISE: FROM SIMILE TO ANALOGY**
>
> *'He was like a toad on our first date ...'*
>
> In 150 words or less, and either in poetry or in prose, expand a simile or metaphor into an analogy. (Use the above prompt if it helps.) As you write, create more and more connections to the image so that it becomes a narrative in its own right.

We can easily fall prey to over-explanation in terms of our images and comparisons, but sometimes it is necessary to extend an image or metaphor in order to make the connection work:

Life is like a box of chocolates. (simile)
You never know what you're gonna get until you open it. (analogy)

Allegories are stretched-out versions of analogies. And they work well for specific purposes, especially when we're trying to get a political or social message across to our readers.

Plato's 'Allegory of the Cave', for example, begins with an image of men in chains. They sit at the back of a cave, by the dim light of a flickering fire. They are forced to watch shadows cast by puppets on a wall behind them. These men are convinced that what they're seeing and experiencing is real life.

We can make this analogous to the idea that this is how people are brainwashed in society by the media.

But Plato goes further, extending the analogy to allegory. He tells the story of one man in the cave who breaks away, escapes into the full bright sun and sees the 'light' of the real world. He realizes that everything in the cave is just a bad copy of reality. Then he has to return and persuade the people inside that they are mistaken, deluded about their beliefs. When he returns and tries to convince his fellow prisoners that they are not seeing the real world at all, but a copy of it, his ideas are seen as so disturbing that he is put to death.

In this allegory, the story stands for another story: that of Socrates who was put to death for trying to show people the truth about reality; it also illustrates Plato's theory that this world is just a shadow of the real spiritual world outside our perceived apprehension of material reality.

Many novels are allegories: the classic *Animal Farm* by George Orwell is one. The trick is that the story must work on two levels. An allegory is just a sophisticated comparison, an extended 'like' device, making something (e.g. a series of events or experiences) similar to something else. So, why do we need these comparisons?

Images are the tools we employ to create layered virtual realities where a reader's experience is both rich and real. Emotional verisimilitude is the result of mental transportation, where all the sensory and motor details elicit responses in the brain that are as real as if the reader experienced those things first-hand. Aside from comparisons being a much more effective way of 'showing' and not telling, they are the means by which we beam our readers into our alternate universes.

Symbols, Dreams and the Power of the Single Image

If we dream of our teeth falling out, what does that mean? What about if we dream of snakes? Lions? In the realm of dreams, symbols appear everywhere. There are thousands of websites devoted to interpreting dreams based on the symbols that appear in them. In fact, for each of us our dream symbols can represent uniquely different things, depending on a million individual elements relevant to the dreamer.

A symbol is a looser comparison between an abstract experience and a concrete (or literary) representative. Whereas a simile, metaphor, analogy or allegory has a direct relation and correspondence, a symbol can have many.

How we use symbols in our writing is up to us. The beauty of a symbol is that once we have established its power, it allows us to say things beyond our words, and to evoke reactions. When we use symbols, we have to know, though, that if we don't imbue our symbols with meaning at the beginning, how a reader interprets symbols could vary wildly as a result of cultural dispositions. For example, a cross is a symbol, but although for some it may mean sanctity, faith and suffering, to others it will represent oppression, narrow thinking or even white supremacy.

But there are some universals, and those often become clichés, for example, the heart symbolizing love, and the skull and crossbones symbolizing danger. But those symbols are explicit, and writers can use or create explicit or more implicit symbols to represent certain experiences. Here's an example in which the symbol is already coded – given its power – so that when it appears, the reader knows its significance:

> My indigenous friend in Australia told me that when I see that eagle overhead, that will be the messenger, the message from my dead father to say, hey, I'm looking out for you.

> We got lost along the headland. Fine mist reduced visibility to nothing. Wind blew cold beneath our shirts and froze us. Hours – or could it have been days? – went by. And then, a gap in the clouds. The sun peeping through, and in its halo, a wide-tailed raptor, circling, watching, brown wings holding the air as it led the way through the dissipating fog.

WIDE-TAILED RAPTOR EXERCISE

1. In 100–150 words, write a poem or piece of prose in which you allow a symbol to emerge.

or

2. Write a short allegorical fable (animals are okay as characters), in which there is a correlation between the events of the fable and current political or social events, and in which characters represent current politicians or celebrities.

Becoming the Master (or Mistress) of Allusions

Allusion is a highly sophisticated comparison, a type of shorthand, comparing the known with the unknown without having to spell it out, though allusions to current events will always date, and then the allusion gets lost:

'He danced like Michael Jackson' – is a simile, but also an allusion. Some readers now will be able to imagine the kind of dancing the allusion refers to. In several decades, the connection may well be lost.

PAUL

This simile enables me to use two words instead of having to describe a whole dance sequence where my character twirls, grabs his crotch, gives a high-pitched squeal and moon walks.

Even 'moon walk' itself is an allusion, which thankfully I do not have to describe. An allusion is a code word.

Allusions, though, have to make use of common cultural comparison; otherwise, the reader will not 'get' them.

I used to teach to my students a Richard Brautigan story, 'The Kool-Aid Wino' (1967: 8), where one allusion did not work:

'Bertrand Russell could not have said it better.'

No one in the class knew who Bertrand Russell was, so the students had no idea how he 'said it'.

How did he say it? Like a wise philosopher who lived in the early twentieth century, with a gravelly voice and ponderously long sentences.

But having to explain an allusion is as bad as having to explain a joke: if you don't get it instantly, it's not worth telling.

Deconstructing Metonymy and Synecdoche

These are comparison devices where we simply replace the word (another shortcut) with another. *Synecdoche* means 'simultaneous understanding' and is a technique where we use a part to refer to a whole.

'Nice wheels, man!' (Your car is awesome).

The prime minister has ruled out 'Boots on the ground.' (The prime minister won't send soldiers to fight on the actual land.)

Metonymy substitutes a thing or concept with something closely associated with it. For example:

> The pen is mightier than the sword. (The power of the written word is stronger than force.)
> The White House (meaning the US government)

Why use metonymy and synecdoche in writing? Why use allegory and analogy? Or figurative language at all? There are those writers who are suspicious of 'flowery' comparisons and prefer to stick to the supposed one-to-one correlation of simple words to things. But the elevation of the literal, the mundane correspondence of one to one is why. Words are slippery, and playing with them in this way is the jazz saxophonist's style, breathtaking skill and versatility, where he shows off what his or her instrument can do for our listening pleasure.

Hysterical Hyperbole

Hyperbole has its place. It's useful for creating images that startle us or tickle us into laughter. Hyperbole pushes description to the extreme and gives us free rein to ramp up the temperature of a reader's reaction.

> 'I've told you a million times not to exaggerate!'

Often hyperbole is a humorous way of communicating something:

> She had like a million zits on her face, man. But I was hardly one to talk. I had these canyons in my face where I had excavated. It was an open cast mine where I had dug out and squeezed and purged and scoured.

GO FIGURE EXERCISE

Using any or all of these – allusion, metonymy, synecdoche, hyperbole – write a paragraph of 150–200 words that conveys a transcendent or intense experience you have had.

Clichés: The Classic Route to Ruining Good Writing

From the French 'stamp', a cliché is the stamping of the same fixed expression onto our page. Instead of writing something fresh, we resort to stamping a worn-out expression.

Clichés were once innovative similes or metaphors which have now become part of common language. 'Bomb rocks Durban' may have once been a journalist's clever metaphor, but now it is what all bombs do.

It is easy to tell if we are using clichés or not. If someone were to say 'I was as white as a …' and we can easily complete the sentence ('a ghost', 'a sheet'), then it is a cliché. Clichés are easy as pie; writing new figurative expressions are not.

Classic cliché example:

> It was all in a day's work, but also just another nail in his coffin. He finished the manhole he'd been digging (to China) and thought, 'Well, another day, another dollar'. He'd been doing the same shit on different days for twenty-one years now, because he'd believed his father's words – that there was no such thing as a free lunch. And anyway, he wouldn't want to be one of those losers who just sat at home, twiddling his thumbs.

CLICHÉ EXERCISE

Choose a cliché, perhaps one found in your own writing, and rewrite it freshly. Or rewrite the above classic cliché example.

The Sensations of Our Senses

Brought up on TV and social media, we are trained on a daily basis to rely on only two of our senses for our information about the world. We perceive our reality and describe it, reliant mostly on what we see and hear. Since we experience so much of our reality through media and devices, our senses of smell, touch and taste aren't engaged. Unless we walk past an overflowing sewer, or the smell of lemony jasmine blossoms assaults our olfactory cells on a spring morning, smell doesn't get our attention. Also, English has few words for these senses, and this makes it difficult to accurately describe the sensations of smell, taste and touch. We rely on limited adjectives such as *bitter, sweet, sour, aromatic, savoury, hard, soft* and *silky*.

But those lack specificity. If we want a visceral quality to our writing, we have to make new metaphors and unique comparisons to do our neglected senses justice in the literary realm.

Example:

> Giving birth was like being slowly impaled on a ten-centimetre red-hot iron that burned and seared its way through her flesh, while some numbskull who had never done this before said, 'Breathe my dear, breathe.'

or

> The gas poured out of the natural vent in the earth and smelled like a thousand farts.

or

> It tasted bright and acidic and made his cheeks want to meet on the inside of his mouth.

> **THREE NEGLECTED SENSES EXERCISE**
>
> Write a 50-word paragraph using one or more of the three neglected senses. How did something taste, smell or feel to touch?

More Than Believable Backdrops: Establishing a Worthy Setting

Setting is commonly seen as the backdrop to character and plot in our narratives. But it's more accurately like the water that fish swim in. And it therefore must be life-giving.

A setting that isn't simmering with portent of one kind or another will leave readers cold. Setting that relies on large blocks of meandering description for its own sake will lose readers quickly, have them skipping to where they can locate the narrative flow again.

Narrative realms don't have to be built tree by tree or furniture item by furniture item. A setting is most effective when it emerges by the way. In a stage play, an armchair, a coffee table and a lamp will suggest a living room. No need to bring in the sideboard, grandfather clock, skirting board and bay window. Flaubert advised that if we hang a rifle on the wall in the first scene, it must go off by the third act. It's exactly the same for the writer of fiction. And non-fiction. And most especially, poetry. We shouldn't have anything superfluous in the scene, because we create reader expectations with every item we describe. If there is a storm at the beginning of the story or poem, it must serve a purpose. It can create the mood of the scene, or counter the mood of the scene, and setting can itself be an active protagonist or antagonist in the narrative. Here's an example from Shelley's non-fiction work in progress:

> The night Nellie arrived, rain blanketed Johannesburg. The Jukskei River, just a hundred metres from the house, roared in flood.
> I closed all my bedroom windows, even the two small ones. Thieves and murderers loved storms. A loud crash of thunder could mask breaking glass. Distant rumbles could hide the sound of a crowbar bending open a security gate, for those rich enough to have one. Besides, open windows at night were simply an invitation for someone less fortunate than you to stick a long pole with a sharp end through the gap and hook things out of your room: your blanket, your pillow, your new watch (a recent present for your eleventh birthday). You had to think of these things.

In this example, there is no expository lump taking care of the fact that there is a storm raging around the house and that the protagonist is afraid. And yet those details emerge as part of the story. Learning to paint literary pictures this way can be fun and empowering.

THREE ITEMS SETTING EXERCISE

Write a paragraph of 150 words that establishes an evocative setting by referring to three elements or items only.

The Magic of Movies

So, we know that as writers we borrow analogously from films, perhaps now more than ever. In our previous section, 'Angling for a View,' the camera angle was related to point of view, and now, extending that, we can add more angles in the interest of finding the best way to establish a setting for any creative piece.

Establishing shot: The wide, or bird's eye view establishes exactly where the reader/viewers are geographically: some films begin with an aerial shot of the town or a panorama of the mountain.

Similarly, a subtitle may establish time or place or both: New York, 1922.

We do this in our writing, sometimes without even being aware.

The *medium and close-up shots* typically frame a character to show how he or she reacts to an environment.

Film techniques writers like to borrow include the *zoom, pan, tilt, cut, fade in/out* and *dissolve*. These are used to change scenes or to switch from a long shot to a close-up view, or vice versa.

Zooming in or out brings the viewer/reader closer to or further from the subject. How we could use this device in writing is by describing a setting from a distance and then focusing on more and more intricate details: the forest, the tree, the leaves, the severed ear lying on the ground, the ants crawling on the ear.

Panning is moving from left to right or right to left in order to reveal setting. We could describe the setting sequentially, imitating the way a person would survey a setting, for example, opening the door, looking at the left of the room, and slowly describing everything in our path until we reach the right side of the room.

Tilting is going from top to bottom, or from down to up.

These devices can be dramatically effective if we are revealing something slowly, or anticipating. For example, we are directed to first see the sky, then lower our eyes down, down, down until we see the corpse at our feet. In the following example from my novel *Cokcraco*, I found it difficult to describe the room all at once and so used the technique I had seen in the beginning of *Back to The Future*, where the camera (in this case the narrating 'I') follows the meandering of the person entering the room.

> The inside of the cottage was a different place to the grimy vision from outside. The chair was covered with the same grainy cockroach design. I turned to the small mat on the floor; the chest of drawers; the lampshade. The bookcase, the sofa – all were cockroach covered. I scrutinised each item in turn. Each cockroach had been hand-picked for size then painted with sweeping blue, green, brown, pink, then varnished and glued neatly into place. The chair was covered in baby cockroaches; the bookcase large, coarse ones;

and the mat, hardy monsters. I stopped at the desk in the centre of the room. On the top was an open book – a journal. A computer screen and keyboard had been pushed to the back, and on the side I saw an old Olivetti typewriter, a sheet of paper in its jaw. I brushed my hands over the paintings, the walls, the furniture, then finally gazed at the Bantu portrait itself. And finally understood. (Williams, 2013: 173)

The *cut* simply throws the viewer from one scene to another and he or she is expected to figure out that the scene has changed. We can indicate this in writing either by starting a new paragraph, leaving a line of space or using dots, stars or some other decorative way to indicate that we are now moving along.

The *fade* and *dissolve* are difficult to use in writing, but are gentler ways of transitioning. Perhaps the equivalent in writing is this kind of dissolving transition:

Meanwhile, while Uncle Ted is wrestling with his problems, back on the farm, George is busy with his own problems.

Here is another example where I used the establishing shot, zoomed in, cut, cut back.

9:30 p.m., 14 June 1986

Saturday evening, both Magoo's and the adjacent Why Not bar on Marine Parade are packed like cattle trucks on the way to slaughter houses. (I hate discos – the smoke, the crowds, the late nights, but I am caught up in something bigger than myself.) This is what I do on Saturday nights. This is where we meet – Sean, Gina, Janet, Alan, Caryn – sensitive white intellectuals, anti-Apartheid activists, all of us.

See, that's me, John, dancing in a circle with Caryn, Gina and Sean. Sean in his tight blue jeans and Durban floral shirt thrashes about wildly, eyes shining, a bottle of Castle beer in his hand. His shaved head bobs above the crowds.

The car crawls along Marine Parade and slides into a parking space right in front of Magoo's. The passenger sweats. 'Don't stop so suddenly, the bomb will go off, man.'

The driver takes a slow puff of his cigarette, pulls the handbrake up. 'It won't go off until we want it to.' (Williams, 2012)

> **MOVIE CAMERA EXERCISE**
>
> Write a 100-word paragraph that establishes a setting. Decide which positions to use: is this scene being set by using an establishing shot, long shot, close-up, zoom, pan, tilt, fade, cut, etc.?
>
> Read the piece out loud and ask fellow writers to comment on which shot the scene is analogous to.

Exterior Landscape as Mirror of the Interior

At its most banal, the exterior scene of a poem, short story, novel, memoir is a basic backdrop against which a narrative plays itself out. And this happens between book covers the world over. But let's explore setting as a compelling device, the agent we use to reflect the interior state of a character, to create mood, to draw readers into our realities.

Author John Gardner (1926–2007) suggested exercises that look at the setting or backdrop through the eyes of a character who has just had something dramatic (and unexplained) happen. The setting becomes the ultimate mirror or metaphor for a character's emotional state.

For example, how does a landscape or a lake appear to a murderer who has just committed a crime? How does the same lake look to a woman whose disgusting husband has just died? The trick, of course, is not to mention the murderer or the death of the disgusting husband, but to let the character's observations reveal his or her disposition … to allow the landscape then to reflect the inner state and allow the emotion to seep in through the perception of the exterior world (Gardner, 1984: 203).

> **MIRROR LANDSCAPE EXERCISE**
>
> Describe a walk through a forest, alongside a stream, from the point of view (first, second or third person – whichever works) of a character who has just done one of the following:
>
> - Committed a crime
> - Had a miscarriage

- Won the lottery
- Found out about a cheating partner or spouse

Let the environment reflect the inner state of the character without ever stating anything explicit. Feel free to use adjectives, adverbs and verbs that enhance the setting, but try not to lapse into overwriting.

or

- Describe an object (e.g. a pen, a watch or a ring) belonging to a dead loved one without ever mentioning the deceased person.

SHELLEY

For me, creating a setting that is immediately a reflection of something deeper and subtextual has been an instinct since I first began to write. It's still so mysterious to me how I can be lying on my bed reading in a weird and uncomfortable position, absorbed by some fictional setting, totally unaware of my actual surroundings, not hearing my son talking to me or the loud army helicopter flying low over the roof, because I'm at a fictional dinner party in which someone is about to be murdered on a rain-drenched balcony, and until I know why that wet night seems so sinister, I must keep reading. Playing with metaphors, reinventing language, creating worlds that others can get into – I live for that, I guess. For me, imagery is the language of the soul, and by soul I mean the territory of self that feels and senses everything not explicit, not stated, not even material.

FURTHER READING AND RELEVANT EXAMPLES

For information on how the brain uses figurative language, please see Annie Murphy Paul's 'Your Brain on Fiction'.

For over-the-top 1960s figurative experimentation, read any of Richard Brautigan's novels, in particular *Trout Fishing in America*.

John Gardner's *The Art of Fiction* is a classic 'how-to' writing book by one of Britain's finest thriller writers.

8
Those Who Speak: Avatars, Characters, Selves

> **Freewrite #8**
>
> *'This is the most important thing I'm ever going to say,' she said ...*

Jahare is a ten-foot-tall fire mage. Inna is a small green elf with a quick mind and a warped sense of humour. For two long earth years they have fought dragons, made narrow escapes and grown to trust and understand one another.

Night. The ice-dragon lies dead at Jahare's feet and he stands victorious outside a cave beneath a rising moon.

'You put your life in danger!' she says. 'You could have been killed.'
'It was my pleasure.'
'Jahare ... '
'What?'
'I'm scared right now.'
'But you've just been saved!'
'I know. It isn't that. I'm afraid I'm falling for you.'
'Ha-ha.'
'It's not funny!'
'No. Sorry. It's cool. So I'm going all out here, Inna. Would you give me your phone number? And your earth-name. ☺ *Please!*'

This isn't high fantasy. It's virtual reality.

Every month, thousands of real people in the real world meet avatars and characters created by other real people in other places, and get to know them and, according to their own admissions, fall crazily and hopelessly in love with virtual constructs.

Is it possible to know someone without having met the person? What about loving someone?

Aside from online dating sites, gaming sites are a popular and populous arena for people to meet up, people who spend most of their time in virtual reality anyway. But in such a world, who exactly are they meeting? We know all too well how easy it could be to fall for an online persona who is shady in real life, or who doesn't actually exist, *but* what an incredible phenomenon that we can meet someone through mere written dialogue (and virtual actions) and come to love them!

And why not? We've fallen in love with characters before. Mr Darcy in *Pride and Prejudice* is over 200 years old, and he still has an infatuated following of young and old women who devour his every word and action. Jane Austen has created a man of worth, who speaks beyond the text, beyond time and across generations. At some level, when we write, we are playing God, and we want others to love and understand our creations.

Being a writer is addictive in the sense that being an actor or a director might be addictive: we get to inhabit different selves, draw on different parts of ourselves and make characters out of nothing except the ephemeral substance of our imaginations. If we feel like acting or speaking or being a different way, characters afford us the opportunity to be multiple selves on any given day. Each persona (Latin for 'mask') we create is a synthesis of our brushstrokes and delineations, and a reader's emotional and image-rich investment in those clues that emerge in the narrative. And this is true whether we're at work creating online avatar versions of ourselves in which we are two feet tall, blue in colour and have made up names; or creating the ultimate love-worthy heroine in a romance novel.

Being Many Characters

PAUL

I create characters out of me. They're all inside autobiographically. I look deep to find them. For example, my YA novel Parallax *has three main characters: an eleven-year-old Australian boy in a small mining town; his best friend, a boy who has only one year to live; and a fiercely independent girl with a million freckles. I never was an eleven-year-old Australian boy in a small mining town. But I was an eleven-year-old boy in a small mining town in Africa. And I had to go back in time to bring that person here to write the book, to show how he feels about the world, to explore his eccentric logic and actions, to show his unrequited love, his fears and his physical appearance. I used me.*

But even the other characters in the novel represent me. The paralysed boy Gustave is the me that felt powerless and frustrated. The girl is another side of me. I gave her my freckles and my caustic tongue.

Characters become loveable, memorable, quotable through their dialogue, their actions and perceptions, and through the eyes of others. If we think about the most followable or unforgettable character we've ever 'met', we can probably highlight exactly why we find the character so memorable. We can admire how the author constructed this individual and pinpoint the actions and situations that revealed and tested the person's character.

Revealing Character through Dialogue-Driven Narrative

Let's acknowledge that as writers, dialogue is one of our most valuable tools to divulge who our characters are and to make them empathetic. This is the use of explicit 'voice' in writing, and characters can rise to immortality or fall into obscurity on this basis alone. Of course, this applies to fiction as well as creative non-fiction and is ultimately a quintessential aspect of the overall voice of a piece. Here's an example from Shelley's memoir *Whisperings in the Blood* in which a conversation between two people in 1938 is reimagined.

- *Where are you going?* she asks him.
- *Johannesburg,* he says. *The city of gold. I'm already ecstatic at the thought of leaving miserable, God-forsaken England forever. And the talk of war is enough to make anyone quite sick. What about you, Miss Frank from Cleveland, Ohio?*
- *I'm going to South Africa to marry the man who's paying my passage over.*
- *Oh well, that's a pity!*
- *What, that I'm going to South Africa?*
- *Nope! That you're planning to marry a man who's simply paying your passage. I'll pay your passage!*
  She laughs. *Too late.*
- *Well, if you don't like your husband-to-be, I'll offer to wait as a replacement.*
  Bertha laughs again and looks away at the night sky. She has never seen stars like this. They go all the way down to the far horizon. They are so bright they look almost within reach.
- *Jokes aside, Bertha. That's rather a brave thing to do.*
- *Yep, I guess so.* (Davidow, 2016: 88)

SHELLEY

This is a how I imagine the dialogue might have evolved between my grandmother, Bertha, and a young man, Harold, who met on a ship from Southampton to Johannesburg in 1938. I have a photo of both of them on the deck of the ship. He has his arm casually around her shoulders, and she looks like she's mad about him. I have pages from her diary in which she reveals that 'he asked, poor fellow.' She must have been referring to a marriage proposal. I wanted to reveal Harold as someone who wasn't just a cardboard background figure, even though he only exists on a few pages of the story. So I've tried to capture the essence that appears in the photo: he seems confident, funny, kind and genuine – a guy any young girl could easily fall in love with.

> **CHARACTER THROUGH DIALOGUE EXERCISE**
>
> Write an exchange between two characters in which you reveal
>
> 1. their relationship to one another;
>
> 2. their characters; and
>
> 3. part of a plot.
>
> Avoid as much as possible 'she said/he said', and keep exposition to a minimum. Let the direct speech do all the work of moving plot along, showing who the characters are and what their relationship is.

The Mechanics of Dialogue: Avoiding Some Classic Deadeners and When It's Time to *Be* the Punctuation Police

When dialogue is smooth, our eyes fly over the page, and we don't even think about it, and before we know it characters reside in our imaginations, looking and sounding as real as people we've met. But when the dialogue is stilted or interrupted, or the characters natter on inanely without a point, an entire narrative can tumble to a standstill.

The over-writing of speech tags also gets in the way of narrative flow. A speech tag is the 'he said' phrase that tells our readers who is speaking. Use speech tags sparingly. They're often not even necessary. Sometimes, readers who are on the hunt for replacements for 'she said' get lost in overwritten substitutions that don't do anything for the characters themselves.

Again, this is not to say that no reader will ever find ridiculous speech tags, stilted, inane or pointless dialogue in bestsellers, but for us lovers of language, our comfort lies in the probability that those characters won't still be living in the minds and hearts of readers very far into the future!

Here are some examples of classic dialogue destroyers:

Adding '-ing' verbs that over-explain or deaden the words preceding the description can really ruin a good moment.

> 'I told you before I don't want to go pack fish in Alaska,' he said, rolling his eyes.
>
> 'I know, and I understand exactly why,' she said, nodding her head and looking out the door. 'But we need the money,' she whispered, sniffing and turning sideways to catch his eye.

If we lose all those cob-webby words sticking to the dialogue, we will be left with a clean, character-revealing interaction.

And another classic error:

> 'Well, I'm going there,' he smiled.

(He can't smile the words – he can say them and then smile.)

The simplicity of 'she said' is preferable to fancy descriptions that draw attention to themselves, because we want the reader's eye to focus on what's being said rather than on a laboured explanation of how it's being said. We're better off 'showing' in the dialogue than 'telling' in the speech tag. Most readers skip speech tags: they are used only to signify who is speaking. And so most of the time, we do not need them anyway because the writer has established who is speaking. The speech tags in the below example are redundant in that they repeat what is already stated in the dialogue and could therefore be omitted to create a more effective exchange.

> 'I hate you,' he snarled viciously.
> 'Ditto,' she spat.
>
> 'I hate you.'
> 'Ditto.'

Being a Dialogue Diva on Punctuation and Speech Tags

There are probably no limits as to how innovative and exceptional we can be in terms of form (and more on this in chapter 10), but in general fiction and non-fiction, consistency in presenting dialogue is the key to clarity and fluid reading. Regarding formatting, following these rules will ensure clarity:

If we use 'he said/she said', we should do that at certain break points in the dialogue, ideally, right at the beginning, right at the end or bang in the middle.

If we use inverted commas, then every bit of dialogue should look like this:

> 'You never listen to me!' he cried.
> 'Listen, Buck. I saw that mouse peep out of your shirt collar,' his mother said. 'You can't take a mouse to school with you, okay?'
> 'He helps me,' he responded, 'with my work.'
> 'What?'
> 'He does! He whispers all the test answers in my ear.'

Dialogue is indented consistently every time a new person speaks. Quotation marks go outside the punctuation. Commas, exclamation marks, and question marks don't require us to use capitals after closing quotes, because the full stop at the end signals the end of the sentence. In the fourth line, the speech tag ('he responded') interrupts a sentence, so use a comma, not a full stop.

In some styles, like the extract from *Whisperings in the Blood*, an author chooses to use italics for dialogue. An author might choose double quotation marks, depending on the country the book is being written in. The rules are the same: just be consistent, and of course when submitting work, check the publisher's requirements. Every time a new person speaks, start a new line. These are basics but often are mishandled, leading to potentially good writing ending up in an editorial slush pile.

Too Much Verisimilitude in Dialogue

Dialogue that relies heavily on our attempts to recreate a fully accented English of one kind or another can irritate readers and make prose incomprehensible or difficult to read. Also, it draws attention to itself. Yet we want our characters to sound unique. There is a continuum between the textbook-correct 'King's English' and street-savvy verisimilitude, and we need to know where to place our characters on it.

Rather than writing a character's entire verbal interaction in a thick Scottish or New Jersey or any other accent, a simple word or two will suffice to give a sense of how a character speaks. The Scottish guy might just throw in a few words like 'the wee lad', and that should be clue enough. The same goes for slang. Use words that represent the character's way of speaking like flavourings in a favourite recipe.

Contractions

The same goes for contractions. We don't, of course, speak in fully pronounced words, so of course we can imitate this in dialogue, for example 'can't' or 'don't'. But if we go overboard (*y'all ain't goin'*), readers will simply skip the dialogue until something more familiar catches their eye.

Misspellings

Misspellings can be used to suggest how people speak, but use them sparingly, so it's evident they're deliberate. Also, be consistent. So if a character says 'muvva', always use that spelling for that character. For example, in *The Color Purple* Alice Walker has the character Miss Celie use 'kilt' for killed, and 'mens' for men.

Bad Grammar

When writing in the voice of foreign characters, be careful not to patronize, stereotype or make characters sound stupid.

Giving Characters Life

It is possible to thoroughly bury a character in clothes, mannerisms and gestures. The result of this can be tedium or, entertainingly, comedy:

> Her high collar, made of blue velvet almost touched her ears. The bun on the top of her head was so tight it pulled her eyebrows up by a good inch, making her look constantly surprised. Her gloves, made of the finest cream silk, fitted her slim hands and shone in the lamplight. Each glove had a small rabbit embroidered onto the pallid material. A too-tight belt pinched her waist, and her eyes blinked slowly as a result of the heavy green eye-shadow.

That character is certainly alive, but there's too much of her. She's an overwritten creation and would do well for herself as the star of a comedy or a piece that is loaded with irony of one kind of another.

Charles Dickens is probably one of the most successful creators of memorable characters (though some say they were exaggerated caricatures, or cartoon portrayals of people). But his techniques are worth examining. In *Oliver Twist*, he describes the Artful Dodger with a few telling brushstrokes: 'as dirty a juvenile as one would wish to see ... (with) all the airs and manners of a man... . All decked out in clothes much too large for him' (Dickens, accessed 23 April 2016).

Perhaps the most obvious thing to say is that characters are not people. They are avatars. We cannot construct whole three-dimensional people in stories or poems or creative non-fiction. At best, we can offer suggestions, sketches, and the more subtle they are, the more opportunity our readers have to use those guidelines to build a character – first out of dialogue, and then description – who lives a vibrant imaginable life in an alternate reality.

When we make characters, we need to provide some 'concrete' and 'significant' detail. Elements of physicality that are perceived by the senses, like too-large clothes, have great connotative power. Detail that is central to meaning-making can be symbolic and have power to transport readers into the 'reality' of a character.

ARTFUL DODGER EXERCISE

Create three characters (60 words for each one) by careful revelation of detail. Use brushstrokes of description that may have symbolic significance later. The objective is to make a strong impression, not build a persona item by item.

Although character lies at the heart of fiction and is essentially any story's emotional centre, there's no evidence as yet that well-delineated characters engage us emotionally any more than one-dimensional characters. It seems to be that when an author creates a one-dimensional character, readers just fatten him up in their imaginations and fill in details that are not provided. In fact, one-dimensional characters can propel the momentum of a page-turning thriller where plot pulls readers from one crash-and-burn moment to the next. But: three-dimensional characters drive narratives in more subtle ways. Because they are more complex and even contradictory, they are easy to relate to. We feel like we see ourselves in them, and in history's record, those are the characters who capture imaginations and live on way beyond the lives of their creators.

So, if we want to create characters who might survive into another century, what can we do with our words? We can 'show' who these 'people' are – using several explicit elements.

What He Thinks, What She Believes: The Inner Lives of Characters

Here's a thought: identifying with the inner 'soul' of a character is the only way in this world we can ever truly inhabit another, see the world through someone else's eyes, and as Harper Lee writes in the classic novel *To Kill A Mockingbird:* 'you never really know a man until you stand in his shoes and walk around in them' (Lee, 1988: 31).

Of course that goes for knowing women, children, mythical creatures and animals too. Or at least, being given the closest imaginal approximation. In writing that transports us into the world of a complex character, readers have a unique opportunity to look at the world through that character's eyes – to become someone else. So, how does the writer reveal the inner life, the emotional and soul disposition of a character?

A simple tactic is to deliver the character's worldview in a way that supports the momentum of the plot. These are the first paragraphs in *Lights Over Emerald Creek*, a speculative young adult fiction by Shelley:

> At sixteen, Lucy believed she was a pragmatic realist – but what she'd seen just over twenty-four hours ago defied all logic.
> It was so deeply inexplicable that it had made the difference between wanting to die – and wanting to live. (Davidow, 2013: 1)

So in the space of just a few words, the reader can know a lot about Lucy: that she's sixteen, that she's seen something that has disturbed her down-to-earth pragmatism and that she's been contemplating suicide. We can show a character's dispositions and views on the world without having to give the explanation that's just been given.

> **WALKING AROUND IN ANOTHER'S SHOES EXERCISE**
>
> Write a paragraph or two (50–100 words) of character description in which you touch on a few essentials about the nature of this person (age, disposition, how he or she thinks and feels about the world). Use first or third person.

Taking Action

In imaginative worlds, as in this world, characters are revealed as much by what they do as by what they say and look like. Actions sometimes speak much louder than words. If a character pulls out a gun and aims it unexpectedly at his best friend, that tells the reader precisely how trustworthy, stable and dependable he is without the narrator having to explain that he is not at all trustworthy, stable or dependable. If a character sits on the grass, digging her fingers into the earth, she may be showing more than the desire to be a farmer sometime in the future.

> We sat with our backs leaning against the hot metal of the car door. I dug my fingers into the earth and uprooted a clump of grass. 'I thought that over the ten weeks, at least you'd write.'
> 'I was really busy. School exams, everything,' he said. 'I have to get good grades.'
> 'I thought of you every minute of every day.'
> He picked up a stone and threw it at a Coke can in the middle of the road. It missed. 'Shit. I don't know. What do you want me to say?'
> 'It's just so weird, like you don't even want to see me. Is that true?'
> Silence. Another clump of grass. And another. The lawn began to look shabby. Dirt under all my fingernails.
> 'I just can't force myself to be in love with you. I want to have fun and I don't want to be tied down.'
> I buried my right hand in the earthen hole at my side. Then I pulled it out, got to my feet and took the keys out of my pocket. Opened the car door, climbed in and started the engine.
> 'Wait!' He banged on the window. 'What the hell? Where are you going?'
> Pressed the accelerator right into the ground. 0–60 in ten seconds. The roar of the engine in my ears.

> **SHOWING EXERCISE**
>
> Using one of these abstract nouns as a guide to the subject matter of a piece, write a paragraph of 100–200 words in which you show both through dialogue and action, that emotion or theme. Don't explain anything.
>
> Trust
> Betrayal
> Kindness
> Remorse
> Revulsion
> Unrequited love

Direct Exposition Description

Sometimes a bit of direct exposition gives the reader necessary anchors.

> Of course, he didn't have to ever go to the gym or work out to achieve the physique that won him stares down the entire length of the series of open offices. His task was mediocre – delivering lunchtime sandwiches. But he moved like a panther. Every muscle, every movement was under his control. Ten years of throwing concrete bricks onto trucks every afternoon to make ends meet would do that for a guy.

> **DIRECT EXPOSITION EXERCISE**
>
> Write a character description that ties physical attributes to information about the character's past or disposition.

What's in a Name?

We name children and animals with careful thought, but what about characters? Imagine a girl named Ziggy. What would she be like? What about her friend Storme? Names have associative qualities that can be very useful in character creation. We can use names to give a sense of a personality. For example, a character called Rafe would be a good foil for another called Jarek.

SHELLEY

Juliet says in Shakespeare's Romeo & Juliet: *'A rose by any other name would smell as sweet' (II, ii, 1–2). And I have to agree with her. Names mean little to me in terms of christening my characters. I'm actually terrible at it. I struggle to find the right names, and then I come up with so many options that I forget them. I've been known to start out with Lucy in chapter 1 and begin chapter 3 with Zoe. I guess they feel just as sweet regardless of what I call them!*

PAUL

My novel Parallax begins with a description of my protagonist, his name as his defining characteristic:

> Me?
> I'm Danny Anderson. Unfortunate name, but no one calls me Danny. At school they call me wanker or tree hugger or Danny-Wanny.
> Nice place, my school.
> Characteristic features: warts on hands. Dozens of them.
> Favourite superhero: Superboy. I like the Clark Kent alter ego thing. Most of the time, I'm Clark Kent, well 100% of the time, actually, but one day I'll break out. One day. (Williams, 2014: 5)

Habits, Tics, Idiosyncrasies

Dickens intentionally gives each of his main characters a characteristic we can remember him or her by. This characteristic may be an item of clothing, a mannerism, a repeated saying. Think of Uriah Heep, who is always ''umble' (humble), or Mrs Pip who wears her apron as a weapon, as if to say: 'Here I am slaving away in the kitchen all my life for you.'

PAUL

I always give my characters some distinctive identification signature. For example, Gustave in my young adult novel Parallax is obsessed with Stephen Hawking and continually quotes him:

Next up: Gustave – eleven earth years old. Code word Stephen Hawking. He can even do the voice on his computer and knows the scientist's quotes by heart. 'People who talk about their IQs are losers', or 'without imperfection, neither you nor I would exist', or 'when we have solved the problem of the universe we have solved the problem of God.'

He prefaces most of his sentences with 'Stephen Hawking says', though we are beginning to suspect that Stephen Hawking could not have said all of the things Gustave attributes to him, like: 'Stephen Hawking says that one day animals will rise up against their human masters and take over the world.'

Gustave has a hole in his heart. He won't live long, a year tops, his doctor says, so he wants to make his mark on the world. Do something people will remember him by, even if he is bottled up in a crippled body. Stephen Hawking in a wheel chair, only able to speak through a computer, didn't stop him becoming the top scientist in the world. Having a hole in your heart is nothing, he says. (Williams, 2014: 4)

Two of my characters in Cokcraco *have signatures: Professor Zimmerlie keeps scratching his scar, and his colleague keeps spouting apt Zulu proverbs:*

Professor Zimmerlie is dressed in a tight dark suit, white shirt, tie, cufflinks, shiny leather shoes. He is the whitest man you have ever seen. And you mean that literally. He is so white, he looks geckoish. And good god, you stare – try not to stare – at the stitches on his head, scars now, faded pink Frankenstein stitches about two centimetres long, neatly caterpillared across his left temple.

Behind him, another man thrusts out his hand. 'Hi, I'm Mpofu. Thami Mpofu.'

'Pleased to meet you.'

'We Zulus have a saying,' says Mpofu. '*Khotha eyikhothayo* ... The cow licks the one that licks her. John has kindly let me use his office and facilities'. (Williams, 2013: 12)

Bear in mind, though, that Dickens's characters tend towards caricature, and the characters in *Parallax* and *Cokcraco* are also caricatured for effect. It is a simplistic way to create character but can be effective if used in moderation. And quirkiness is always welcome in comedy.

> **CHARACTER QUIRKS EXERCISE**
>
> Write a short scene (100 words) in which a character's quirks or idiosyncrasies are highlighted. Be liberal and have fun. Show, rather than tell. Caricature is fine.

How Others See Them

There is an exercise in self-awareness that helps people see themselves from the outside. Think of how you see yourself, compare this to how others see you and then compare this to how you think others see you. And finally how are you really, outside of your and others' perceptions? The fact is, we reveal only aspects of ourselves to others, and they often misread us or else see things in us we don't see in ourselves.

Jane Austen's novels are based almost entirely on these perceptions of self and others. *Pride and Prejudice* (initially called *First Impressions*) is premised on false perceptions. Elizabeth Bennett's impressions of Darcy, his impressions of her, her sisters' and her mother's impressions of the various suitors, are all based on superficial information. We can be tricked into believing the false impressions one character has of another or tricked by an unreliable narrator's judgement. Mark Twain's Huck Finn thinks himself despicable because he is helping a runaway slave to freedom.

In Paul's memoir *Soldier Blue*, a character is introduced in foreshadow and is only known by the protagonist's mother's favourable impressions:

> But what was most different about the house was that it was occupied by a ghostly intruder, a girl called Willow, whose dressing gown hung on the back of the bathroom door and whose scent permeated the house. I had been warned about her in my mother's letter, but had somehow skimmed over the section that announced this new arrival in our lives.
>
> 'She's very religious, but not in a bad way,' my mother said. 'She holds my hand and prays with me at night – for you, for Bernard, for all the boys in the bush, for our country. I hope you don't mind, Paul, she's staying here in the guest room'. (Williams, 2008: 175)

> **THROUGH ANOTHER'S EYES EXERCISE**
>
> Describe a protagonist through another's eyes. Allow the perceptions and judgements of the perceiving character to reveal things about the protagonist that the reader may otherwise not know.

Character through Juxtaposition and Relationships

This happens in life as it does in literary narratives: one person's disposition and personality contrasts and highlights another's when they are together. Sometimes the juxtaposition of the two characters is favourable; sometimes the contrast is extreme and allows one person or character to come out looking like the better half of the relationship, the friendship, the partnership. Most often, characters, just like people, need each other in order that their own unique traits are highlighted. The classic hero's journey relies on juxtaposition of the hero and the hero's nemesis or enemy. Where the hero may be calm and irreverent in the face of an enemy, the nemesis will succumb to a furious temper. Of course this makes the hero appear far more trustworthy and likeable:

> 'Put down your sword, you coward. Your life is mine whichever way you look.'
> 'Why the hurry? I'd rather fight you first!'
> Gurkye lunged forward, his bloodshot eyes and rotten teeth taking up Samuel's entire vision.
> 'Die, then, miserable man!' The monster's breath burned Samuel's cheeks.
> 'Again,' said Sam. 'Not so fast.'

> **JUXTAPOSITION EXERCISE**
>
> Write a 150-word interaction between two characters who possess contrasting qualities. Show this through dialogue and action.

SHELLEY

I've read books where the characters seem to be wooden puppets that are moved along using invisible strings; I don't last long reading those books. And if I start writing such a character or forcing a character into existence, the narrative usually dies a quick and probably merciful death. In writing both my fictional characters and real-people-based characters in memoir, I strive for authenticity. Would So-and-So say this? Would she do this? Really? And now I have to add my bit on empathy: there's current research by neuroscientists using functional magnetic resonance imaging (fMRI) that demonstrates that people who are emotionally transported during reading fiction develop greater empathy in real life, both immediately after reading pro-social fiction and over time. These readers have greater "Theory of Mind (TOM)" (Bal et al., 2013), which translates as the capacity to empathize. Of course, there is also evidence to show that writers are highly empathetic creatures because they spend so much time walking around in their characters' shoes. (Make books, people, not wars!) It is possible to make the world a better place with our words.

The Evolution of Character: Changes over Time

The best characters in the best stories evolve and change over the course of the narrative. Our commitment to following them is partly rooted in the fact that they start out in one way, face adversity and possibly failure, meet challenges head-on and then change slowly, becoming more courageous, less judgemental, more essentially human. Unless, of course, the story is tragic, in which case this evolution happens in reverse, and adversity breaks someone's spirit and casts the person onto the shore of life without any rescue crew. These, though, are the mirror journeys of our souls. We often read a story because we are fascinated by a character, by his or her choices and struggles. The moment we feel empathy and emotional engagement, we are prepared to follow the character anywhere.

Characters are not static. Those who speak in our narratives grow and change and develop, or decline and rot, or aspire to greatness and fail or succeed. They develop in action, in the momentum that pushes plot forward, in the things they say. Character and plot are intimately intertwined (more on that just a page away): the events in a narrative can propel a character into self-realization (or not), but the character is often the catalyst for the events that drive the plot. As the omniscient creators of our imaginative universes, we place our characters in situations that test them, that goad them into action and put them on a road to transformation that closely resembles our own lived narrative journeys.

CHARACTERS THROUGH TIME EXERCISE

1. Take a memorable page of that favourite dialogue and action, and write a mirror piece that imitates the situation, the style (not the subject matter) with different characters in different circumstances.

2. Then imagine time has passed, and write dialogue that happens between the same characters five or ten years later. Reveal how they may have changed, but ensure they are still recognizable.

FURTHER READING AND RELEVANT EXAMPLES

Read any Charles Dickens novel and you are immediately embroiled in descriptions of characters, their mannerisms, actions, names and manner of speaking. Observe how Dickens puts characters in situations that allow them to reveal who they are.

By contrast, read a Jane Austen novel and you will be given 'impressions' of characters from the narrator's and from other characters' points of view.

9
Building Narratives: Movement through Time and Place

> **Freewrite #9**
>
> *In the dark, he rummaged for the map ...*

We spend much of our lives living in imaginary worlds – worlds of made-up stories and hypothetical situations. Imagination is big business. As a species, we spend so much money on watching the fictional realities created in films that people involved in movie-making live multimillion dollar lifestyles and are treated like gods – their fashions, words and thoughts splashed all over the media. We live in the virtual realities of computer games; we read books, watch TV. And if that is not enough, we then go to sleep and spend all night creating stories in our heads: our dreams are wild fantasies, fictions we create for whatever reason – in short, we are, without a doubt, creatures with a huge hunger and capacity for narrative in any shape or form.

One of the most interesting elements in the universe is the way our brain processes things, works out problems, expunges emotions and deals with grief, loss and so on, through story making. Fiction seems central to our way of seeing the world, vital for our mental health, a necessary device to make sense of our lives and to maintain a balanced emotional life and a sense of self.

Dreams, according to Freud, are the territory of the Unconscious, where our repressed Id, our socially unacceptable desires, lurks. Bottled tightly inside our Ego and Superego, the repressed Id-genie apparently escapes in wisps and whispers, in disguised form, welling up in our dreams, our Freudian slips, our neuroses.

Dreams can be a fascinating resource to writers. They emerge as narratives complete with literary devices such as allusion, metonymy, symbol, metaphor and, yes, omission and elision. But more than that, they reveal that the fundamental way humans make sense of the world is through the construction of plot.

> **ID-GENIE EXERCISE**
>
> Write a 200-word piece inspired by a recent confounding or powerful dream (if you can remember one). Allow the narrative to reveal its hidden subtext.

PAUL

I once dreamed of a man who 'unwrote' the books he appeared to be writing:

> I held a book under my arm and watched intensely as he wrote over words already written. 'These books are for reading,' he said, continuing to write.
>
> He wasn't writing. He was moving his pen across the line of words, yes, but as he wrote, he left empty lines, empty pages behind him, as if his pen was sucking up the ink on the page.
>
> 'I'm not writing, I'm unwriting.'
>
> 'But how selfish! Who else can read that book after you've been … unwriting it? No one.'
>
> 'Finished. Now yours?'
>
> Before I realized what he was doing, he had whisked the book out from under my arm and flattened it open on the desk. 'Wait a minute,' he said. 'These books are blank. You've been reading them.'
>
> 'Yes.'
>
> 'The words are gone. Every word you read disappears. You know that?'
>
> 'No.'
>
> It was true. I paged through the beautiful book and it was now a mere journal, a blank book with faint blue lines. The small print of the copyright page was still on page two – I hadn't bothered to read that – but as I glanced at it, the print began to fade.

End of dream.

I had no clue what this dream was about, and I wrote it as a story. So this places me in the same place as the reader. It has a beginning, middle and end, a plot, characters, a theme, symbolic and figurative meanings and conflict. It demonstrates that we are all storytellers intuitively, even genetically.

Why We Need Conflict

Story (it seems) is about characters overcoming adversity. In the last chapter, we looked at how character is forged through conflict, in overcoming obstacles. In this chapter, we'll see just how much trouble and unhappiness and misfortune we can dump on our characters, and why.

Many of us see ourselves as being on a journey to self-enlightenment, to self-improvement, self-realization, self-actualization, and failing that, ruin and tragedy. That is why we construct stories about good triumphing over evil, light conquering darkness. We can see each individual life as a hero's journey, and story, plot, narrative could be our fundamental psychological way of achieving this. We tell stories of our lives to make sense of them, and create beginnings, middles and ends to order the often-chaotic random events and to smooth them into meaning. It is a story of our desire to achieve something, pitted against the opposing forces of nature, other people and events that try to stop us. Hence 'protagonist' and 'antagonist' 'for' or 'against' the action, or the direction, the motion of the narrative.

That is why conflict, struggle, trouble is interesting. Drama can only occur if there is desire pitted against its adversary, the thwarting of desire.

> Desire + Danger = Drama

> And fiction is the art of human yearning towards something.
> We read books or watch movies to see heroes triumph.
> So in this chapter, we ask you to choose a recent piece of fiction and answer these questions:

- What is the conflict in your narrative?
- What does the main character want, yearn for or desire?
- What danger, trouble or problem exists?
- What does the opening paragraph of your narrative promise?
- How does your ending resolve or answer the problem or question you posed at the beginning?

Intuitive Plotting

We are often taught by creative writing instructors to 'write what we know'. Of course. Personal experience gives validity and authenticity to our writing because we know the details. But writing a story can often be a surprising experience for a writer who only gets to know what happens as the story is being written. E. L. Doctorow (alluded to in an earlier chapter) likens writing this way to 'driving a car at night. You can only see as far ahead as your headlights, but you can make the entire journey that way' (Doctorow, 1986).

SHELLEY

My writing is sometimes as surprising to me as it might be to a reader who has never seen it before. I often write without knowing, feeling my way. The act of writing reveals plots, characters and themes that I might not have consciously thought of. I know I am not alone. Most people who write understand this mysterious process (called 'practice-led research' in academic terms).

So how do we unearth the material used to tell stories, write poetry? How do we plunge into that unconscious, that dream space, and come out with something of value?

Practice-led Research

In the study of creative writing at a postgraduate level, practice-led research is a recognized research method. Conventional research involves investigating a topic, conducting experiments and surveys, gathering data and then writing it up. Creative writers can research their novels this way too, but it is a common research methodology that they do not know what they are investigating until they begin to write, sometimes until after they have written. It is in the writing that they discover what it is they are researching. Somehow the act of writing is itself a research method, a way of discovering truth.

The behavioural psychologist B. F. Skinner recognizes that 'writing is a much more complex act than simply transcribing existing thoughts into words as accurately as possible. The physical act of writing is the cause, not the effect, of new and original thought' (Skinner, 1972: 26). Carlos Fuentes, Mexican novelist, agrees: 'Bad books are about things the writer already knew before he wrote them' (1991). Stephen King uses the analogy of archaeology to describe this mysterious process:

> The best work that I've ever done always has a feeling of having been excavated, of already being there. I don't feel like a novelist or a creative writer as much as I feel like an archaeologist who is digging things up and being very careful and brushing them off and looking at the carvings on them … . The thing is, for me, I never get all that stuff out unbroken. The trick and the game and the fun of it is to see how much of it you can get. Usually you can get quite a lot. (King, 1991)

In this way our writing becomes a quest for knowledge, grappling for words and stories to find out what is in our unconscious. It is okay to begin with uncertainty and write without knowing where we are going. Writing is an act of discovery. There are many exercises and methods to 'get all that stuff out unbroken':

- *Journals*: Keeping a writing journal is a good way to practise writing and to unearth the lost cities of our unconscious.
- *Freewriting*: The exercises at the beginning of each chapter are prompts, but freewriting is also a way of thinking aloud about writing ideas, and a method to wrestle with problems and things that bother us during the day (and night). We write to discover, explore, articulate.

And this idea of writing as discovery is crucial: it separates creative writing from other writing. If essays answer questions, and journalism exposes the 'facts', then creative writing questions or posits problems. Creative writing shows how but does not tell anyone 'why'. It renders but does not have to explain.

And this is perhaps the best way to create depth in writing, avoid the surface trivialities of blandness and give our writing gravitas and resonance.

The Two Subjects

The poet Richard Hugo tells us that when we write poetry (or fiction, or non-fiction), the process of writing will reveal what he calls 'two subjects', or two steps in the making of the final piece:

> A poem can be said to have two subjects, the initiating or triggering subject, which starts the poem or 'causes' the poem to be written, and the real or generated subject, which the poem comes to say or mean, and which is generated or discovered in the poem during

the writing. That's not always true because it suggests that the poet always recognizes the real subject. The poet may not be aware of what the real subject is but only have some instinctive feeling that the poem is done. (Hugo, 2010: 4)

We discover by writing, by playing with words. Hugo gives an example of a poet who decides to write about 'Autumn Rain' and so entitles the poem this, and then tries to find words that fit the initial ideas. Frustrated that she cannot live up to the 'perfect thing', the picture in her mind, she may abandon the poem or the subject. But she must not give up at this point. This is where the real work of writing poetry begins. And ironically, we may have to abandon that triggering subject when we find out what the poem or story is really about.

'The perfect thing' is a phrase Cormac McCarthy used to describe his striving to reach the 'signpost' behind the triggering subject:

> You always have this image of the perfect thing which you can never achieve but which you never stop trying to achieve … . That's your signpost and your guide. You can't plot things out. You just have to trust in, you know, wherever it comes from. (McCarthy, 2007)

SHELLEY

This happens to me quite a lot: I start out with a particular idea and about two-thirds of the way through the book or story or poem, I realize I'm writing about something else. I discover what British/American poet and memoirist Judith Barrington called the 'ghost' in the piece, similar to a paragraph ghost, but not quite the same; it refers in some way to the deeper subject or theme. Once I find that, I know I'm on the right track, though it might mean that I'm heading in a different direction to the one I anticipated at the beginning.

AUTUMN RAIN EXERCISE

Write a poem of 10–12 lines choosing a title that has a seasonal or weather-related theme. Approach it with the disposition needed for a freewrite (relaxed, nothing to prove, no one is going to publish this).

Afterwards, exchange poems with someone else in the group, and discuss whether a plot or second subject (a 'ghost') may be found.

Pyramid Schemes: Formulaic Plotting

The classic plot has been mapped out by Freytag (a nineteenth-century German novelist and playwright) in his triangle or pyramid (1863).

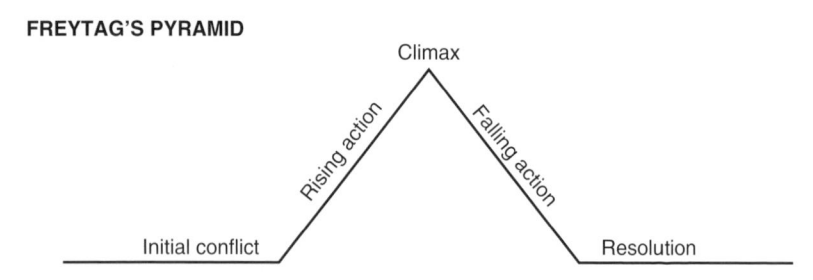

FREYTAG'S PYRAMID

A diagram showing a triangle with "Climax" at the apex, "Rising action" on the left slope, "Falling action" on the right slope, "Initial conflict" at the bottom left, and "Resolution" at the bottom right.

This diagram helps readers to understand narratives and how they work. Most stories fit this archetypal pattern, and it is good for writers to know this. We may consciously or unconsciously follow this formula. Or we may, after writing our narrative, need to structure it and frame it in a conventional way. It seems that this is how the human brain processes and sorts out our narratives.

In this formula, we are always confronted with:

Initial conflict: something gets the story going or puts the characters into conflict and this tension rises and rises (*rising action*) until something has to break, which is the *climax* when it does break, and it then spills over and unravels, de-tenses into the *denouement*, and finally ends with the *resolution*, where everything is sorted.

While we are on the subject of 'the formula', there is a common notion that there are only two plots: a stranger comes to town, and the hero goes on a journey. Or just one plot, depending on whose point of view the stranger's journey is seen from. Motion. Direction. Travel. If there is only one plot, it is this: we take our readers on a journey.

Hero with a Thousand Faces

In 1949, Joseph Campbell gathered stories and myths from numerous cultures across the world and came up with this synthesized archetypal plot: the hero's journey (Campbell, 2008). So successful is this formula that Hollywood uses it over and over, and audiences never tire of it. In the hero's journey, the story is always the same, though settings and characters may change: the hero (or heroine) sets out on a journey that may be physical or metaphorical. He or she has certain powers, either inner strengths or perhaps a supernatural gift. Along the way, at a time when things are getting rough, he or she meets a mentor whose wisdom will be a guiding factor. This wisdom is usually sorely needed because adversity is always just around the corner. No hero's journey is complete without a nemesis – an arch-enemy, or an aspect of self that is determined to undermine the protagonist and which appears to be equally as powerful as the protagonist. Just before our protagonist arrives at a long-sought-for goal, a threshold experience awaits. This is where the hero faces his or her fears, confronts the most difficult challenge of all and overcomes it.

THE HERO'S JOURNEY EXERCISE

We are always the heroes and heroines of our own stories. In answering these questions (a paragraph for each one) the beginnings of a memoir or autobiography may arise. Here's your own life as a hero's journey:

1. What journey or quest are you on?
2. What powers do you have?
3. What mentor will help you?
4. What adversity are you struggling against?
5. What or who is your nemesis?
6. What threshold experience do you face?

Think of a zillion fairytales, of the young adult fantasy series overwhelming the shelves in bookshops everywhere and of the edge-of-your-seat thrillers that tumble off the bestseller slots in those bookshops into our hands. We are tapping into some unconscious mechanism of the human brain which understands the essence of the hero's narrative and how it represents all our stories. We can use archetypal plots as the narrative maps in novels or non-fiction books. Many writers use them. They plot their novels to the exact stages of the hero's journey. In these books we find the classic plot and character archetypes. It's not hard to recognize the mentor, the nemesis, the seemingly unattainable goal or elixir, the classic threshold experience when all seems to be lost … and finally the arrival and resolution at the journey's end. These are formulaic winners precisely because they resonate with the psyche of millions of readers.

And of course we can innovate on the hero's-journey formula. The hero myth can be subverted or extended or made contemporary and relevant to our generation. Questions that may lead to innovations might be:

- Are the archetypal characters to be taken at face value? (Perhaps the hero is really the villain and vice versa.)
- Is the nemesis really always the evil opposition? (Sometimes we are our own worst enemy.)
- Why not have fun by setting up reader expectations and then subverting them? (Fate ensures that we can rarely predict the narrative of our own lives.) Or instead of the resolution at the end being a happy one, what if the storyline is a tragedy, where nothing goes right? (As so often happens, we do not always come out on top in our lives, our narratives.)

Sucking Readers into the Vortex

Plot always begins with a problem, a question or a postulation. A beginning promises something. The writer sets up an unresolvable conflict, or an injustice, and the motion of the story, the journey to the answer or to see justice done, is the reason readers keep reading.

A first sentence, says Stanley Fish, 'is a promissory note. It telegraphs everything that's going to follow … . It has an angle of lean. It leans forward … allowing the unfolding of the sentence to be, in effect, the entire work. If you write a first sentence that has in mind all the sentences that are to follow, it's going to have a particular power' (Fish, 2011).

Examples of some possible first sentences:

> I had spent every waking minute determined that I would never do anything to hurt her … and then the day came when my irrevocable actions precipitated the nightmare.
>
> He had been dead a full twenty-four hours, but this didn't bother him in the least.
>
> Sometimes, she told him, you have to just get out of the way of your own life.

> **LEANING FORWARD EXERCISE**
>
> 1. Read the first sentences of three favourite novels or stories. What makes them 'promissory'? Which way do they lean?
> 2. Look at one of your own stories. Does the first line promise anything or lean in any particular direction?
> 3. Write a first line of a new story or novel that holds a promise – that leans and presents a possible problem or question or hook.

Beginnings and Endings

PAUL

I can never be sure about the first line until I have finished the story. I only know what the story is about once I have finished it.

Beginnings are fiddly things. I advise that once you have written a story, take out the first line or paragraph and see if the omission of the waffling beginning helps. I don't think I have ever used a beginning in my final edit that I wrote in my earlier drafts. Here, for example, is a story I wrote about the Brisbane floods in Queensland, Australia:

> He heard it first, a curious rushing noise. Stopped to listen. He saw it – but still couldn't quite make out what it was, or believe what it was. Then it hit.

The beginning promises to tell us what 'it' is. The story poses the question: how will he survive? Will he? What will happen to him? Who is he? The problem in the opening is similar: how will he live through this flood? It leans towards an urgent action that needs to be taken.

What about two beginnings? If you cannot decide on one, offer two to the reader. Or more. Murray Bail's *Eucalyptus* offers at least five openings. Here are two:

> We could begin with *desertorum*, common name Hooked Mallee. Its leaf tapers into a slender hook, and is normally found in semi-arid parts of the interior... .

> Once upon a time there was a man – what's wrong with that? Not the most original way to begin, but certainly tried and proven over time, which suggests something of value, some deep impulse beginning to be answered, a range of possibilities about to be set down. (Bail, 1999: 3)

J. M. Coetzee offers a 'novel' way to begin a novel, suggesting his unease at having to begin and pulling off his beginning with some linguistic sleight of hand:

> There is first of all the problem of the opening, namely, how to get us from where we are, which is, as yet, nowhere, to the far bank. It is a simple bridging problem, a problem of knocking together a bridge. People solve such problems every day. They solve them, and having solved them, move on.
>
> Let us assume, however it may have been done, it is done. (Coetzee, 2003: 1)

The beginning of Bail's narrative suggests that beginnings are arbitrary and that we could start a story in a number of ways. The beginning of Coetzee's narrative suggests that the beginning is a problem that could be skipped.

Famous Last Words

Endings are the same as beginnings in terms of their importance, and what they do. Often when we're writing our first draft, we don't realize that we've begun too early, that we could cut out the first paragraph or page even, and that this would give us a much punchier beginning. (This is worth a try.) The same is true of endings.

SHELLEY

When it comes to endings, I have learnt finally to stop at the right place! For many years and many narratives, including poems, I knew that even if I thought I'd written a good ending, the chances were high that I'd go back, erase the last line, or even the last paragraph, and find the proper conclusion that way.

It is so easy to end too late and ruin a powerful moment. If we cut out the last line or paragraph, it's worth seeing what happens.

PAUL

For example, here is the original ending to a memoir, another attempt I made, and the same piece with the ending cut out. In the edited version, the narrative ends with a resonant decisiveness. First try:

> We stand. I embrace her, and hold our past in the circle of my arms. And then I let it go. As I walk down the driveway, I feel her watching me from the door. I turn once, and she waves with two fingers, her head to one side, grey-blonde hair cascading over her shoulders. With each step I take away from her, I half-expect her to call me back.
> 'Paul?' I barely have time to turn around and she is in my arms. 'I love you,' she says. 'I have always loved you. And I always will.'

Way too soppy. So I wrote another ending.

> We stand. I embrace her, and hold our past in the circle of my arms. And then I let it go. As I walk down the driveway, I feel her watching me from the door. I turn once, and she waves with two fingers, her head to one side, grey-blonde hair cascading over her shoulders. With each step I take away from her, I half-expect her to call me back.
> She never does. I take three steps, five, ten, and stop myself from looking back. Around the corner, and I begin to cry, I know I will never see her again.

This didn't work either. The final ending was easy: I simply cut both options out and left it to the reader. I did have irate emails asking me what happened, and some whacky interpretations. But what this ending did was make the reader reassess the whole relationship from the beginning to find clues as to what would happen.

> We stand. I embrace her, and hold our past in the circle of my arms. And then I let it go. As I walk down the driveway, I feel her watching me from the door. I turn once, and she waves with two fingers, her head to one side, grey-blonde hair cascading over her shoulders. With each step I take away from her, I half-expect her to call me back. (Williams, 2008: 402)

Of course, there are no rules about how many endings anyone should have in a novel. Keep it open-ended. Give two options, as Dickens had to do with *Great Expectations*, as the public outcry demanded that he rewrite the unhappy ending. Or Fowles's *The French Lieutenant's Woman* (1969). Or more. How about like in Richard Brautigan's *A Confederate General from Big Sur* (1964), which finishes with not one, not five, but 186,000 endings per second?

A FIFTH ENDING

A seagull flew over us. I reached up and ran my hand along his beautiful soft white feathers, feeling the arch and rhythm of his flight. He slipped off my fingers away into the sky.

186,000 ENDINGS PER SECOND

Then there are more and more endings: the sixth, the 53rd, the 131st, the 9,435th ending, endings going faster and faster, more and more endings, faster and faster until this book is having 186,000 endings per second. (Brautigan, 1966: 153)

FAMOUS LAST WORDS EXERCISE

1. Exchange a recent narrative with a writing partner. See if editing out the final line or paragraph makes the piece more compelling.
2. Write alternative endings to a story and try them out on readers.

Moving through Time and Space

Plot is a roller-coaster ride. Once we set a story in motion, it will unravel, unfold, shoot forward in that direction. Or to use another analogy, beginning a narrative is like setting a tiger loose. As long as the tiger leaps forward and doesn't just curl up and lie down, our plot will take us on a wild journey full of unexpected forays into unchartered territories.

Creating Suspense

Readers want to know what happens next, so the most obvious plot technique is to hold back information, make them curious about what will happen. To many storytellers, this is instinctive. 'You'll never guess what happens next!' Unexpected twists, red herrings, surprising back flips are all the ingredients for good writing. Sometimes these occur naturally, but most of the time we have to manufacture them.

In Medias Res

Backstory can be the scourge of any narrative, and in particular fantasy and sci-fi stories because often writers need to create an alternative world or explain the events that have led up to the present time (or future time). And backstory halts the present trajectory of the plot. Of course we want to give readers the background, and sometimes it is necessary for them to know what sort of world they are entering, but many budding writers deaden their story with long-winded descriptions. We can also just as easily lapse into providing a résumé of the character when he or she enters the action: *Sally was twice divorced, had bad experiences with men, and now was considering whether she should ...*

A way to avoid this heavy front-loading of the narrative flow is to start not at the beginning, but *in medias res* (literally – in the middle), and let the reader catch up, guess, work it out. And then slowly drop the backstory in.

Soldier Blue was rejected a number of times because publishers said the beginning was boring. It began with the narrator's birth and went on from there.

> When my parents decided to go to Africa in September 1958, they didn't know they were stumbling into the beginnings of a civil war that would spiral into political madness, and end in economic ruin and poverty. They didn't know that their only son would be coerced into fighting in the war. Nor did they know that in the early hours of the new millennium, they would have to flee the Dark Continent, leaving their house, car, servant, bank account, and forty-six-year-old suntans. (Williams, 2008: 5)

PAUL

I lifted a tense, riveting, shocking part of my draft, where a plane was shot down and the survivors massacred, to begin the book, and then jumped back to the 'I was born' bit. Now readers were hooked and were prepared to follow my life story because they wanted to know how I would get from here to there. The next two publishers both offered me contracts within a week of each other.

> A bang shook the aircraft. It lurched to one side, plunged into a giant air pocket and spun ninety degrees, east to south. The two newly-weds clutched each other and stared out of the starboard window. Flames and smoke poured from the first engine. A metal fragment thunked past. The plane shuddered again, and the second engine burst into flames. Black smoke rushed past the window; intense heat radiated through the thick glass into the cabin. One man drew the blinds. 'Put

your head between your knees and hold your ankles,' another told his wife. The No Smoking and Fasten Seat Belt signs blinked on, and the two air hostesses rushed to the front of the plane. The pilot's first words to the control tower were jumbled. (Williams, 2008: 1)

Flashback

Flashbacks can work really well to provide necessary details, either at the beginning of a narrative or in the middle. They can be used as beginnings if they involve action-filled scenes. They can be left for the middle of the narrative to go back to once the reader is hooked and wants to know about the character. At that point we can afford to take a break from the present narrative and plunge into a past scene that explains the present.

> ### *MEDIAS RES* EXERCISE
>
> Write a beginning paragraph (100–200 words) that lands characters in the middle of the action. Use dialogue, if necessary, to move the plot along. Begin at high speed and keep the pace sustained for all 100–200 words.

Foreshadowing

We never want our readers to sit there thinking, 'Why, exactly, am I reading this? Nothing is happening!' Foreshadowing in images, and plot spoiling, can set up expectations that keep readers glued to the page. Plot spoilers are blatant and can work well to whet appetites. It's hard to resist reading on if the sentence is: 'In a few days he would be dead'. Or: 'Little did she know that this would be the most significant meeting of her life'.

Flashback and foreshadowing both help shape our expectations, and also create pathos. We can see the present in three dimensions: the past, present and future.

Paul uses this device in *Soldier Blue* when his character is about to go off and fight a war.

> The irony, of course, is that three years from now, I would not have had to fight at all. From 1972 until 1978, war was the status quo, and my military service a normal rite of passage. But unknown to me, as early as 1977 the regime was beginning to crumble; by 1978, Smith had been strong-armed into settlement; in 1979, he set in place a moderate

('puppet') black government, which collapsed within six months; and by 1980, the war, the regime, the thousand-year reign was all over. My classmates in intake 155, 156, 157 would take the brunt of the war in casualties, but by 1979, conscription would end and the 'terror war' would be over. Three years from now, the wet street my parents were now crossing to get back to their cars would no longer be called Railway Avenue, but Kenneth Kaunda Avenue, after the Zambian president who assisted our enemy zipra in the war. Those three hundred families sending their boys to fight against zanla's Robert Mugabe, public enemy number one, and now driving back to their white, middle-class suburbs in Hillside, Greendale and Eastlea, would soon have to drive across Robert Mugabe Way and onto Samora Machel Avenue to get home.

And if we were to squint myopically even further into the future, say twenty-five years from now, we would see those same parents smiling with cynical satisfaction at the confirmation of their worst fears and direst predictions about African majority rule. See how these neat roads have degenerated into potholes – this is the Africa up north Smith was warning us about. We were right! Smith was right! The same trains would leave from the same station, but the sidewalks would be lined with war-maimed beggars. Large black families would wait patiently in long queues with plastic bags, goats and chickens, for delayed, overloaded trains; the lavatories would overflow with sewerage; litter would plaster the fence in a solid wall. In twenty years' time the signs Robert Mugabe Way, Kenneth Kaunda Avenue, and Samora Machel Avenue would be gone, stolen for use as coffin handles for the many AIDS victims, and eventually the train itself (yes, the same Garrett articulated loco) would stop running because amateur panhandlers would undermine the tracks on the way to Bulawayo in a vain search for gold. And Mugabe, in his drive for total control, would implement draconian measures of repression: detention without trial, torture, disenfranchisement. In order for his Socialist state to succeed, he would find it necessary to intensify racial hatred and engulf the whole sub-continent in a major conflict, take away civil liberties, gag the press and expel all foreign dignitaries who disagreed with him.

But not now. Not yet. In 1977, the war was still smouldering, and I had to live through this slow-burning chunk of history. (Williams, 2008: 128–9)

Nabokov plot-spoils one of his early novels (*Laughter in the Dark*, 1969) by telling his readers the ending in the first sentence, and then justifies his plot-spoiler by saying that the pleasure in the story is in the telling, not in the 'and then?' race to find out what happened.

Once upon a time there lived in Berlin, Germany, a man called Albinus. He was rich, respectable, happy; one day he abandoned his wife for the sake of a youthful mistress; he loved; was not loved; and his life ended in disaster. (Nabokov, 1989: 1)

Because we know what has happened to our main protagonist, the story is saturated with poignancy and tragedy. We know his mistress is going to ruin his life, so we watch in helpless dread as the story unfolds.

It is up to us as writers to decide whether we want to create suspense or poignancy of a retrospective, fatalistic knowledge.

Cliffhangers

Closing off a chapter with a neat resolution is not always a good thing. The expression *cliffhanger* originated in the early movies, for example *The Perils of Pauline* (1914), where the heroine was literally hanging from a cliff at the end of one episode, and the audience had to wait until the sequel to find out if or how she survived.

Victorian writers such as Dickens and Hardy used this device in their serialized novels to ensure sales of the consecutive publications.

But the original cliffhanger prize must go to Scheherazade in *Tales of the Arabian Nights*. In the story, the sultan takes a new wife to bed every night and chops off her head the next morning. So Scheherazade, the latest wife, schemes to save her life by telling her husband bedtime stories and never finishing them, leaving him in suspense until the next night. He cannot kill her because he wants to find out how her story ends. So each night she cunningly weaves the end of the previous night's story into a new one, which ends on a cliffhanger.

> **CLIFFHANGING, FORESHADOWING, PLOT-SPOILING EXERCISES**
>
> Try at least one of these 200-word exercises:
>
> 1. Write a passage in which you end the section on a cliffhanger.
>
> 2. Write a passage that foreshadows, through use of metaphor, something that will come to pass later.
>
> 3. Write a passage in which you spoil the plot by telling the reader what will happen in the future.

Themes and Hidden Narrative Movements

We normally talk about theme as readers of literature, not as writers. It's part of the vocabulary of analysis. The writer may not know what the theme of her piece is, and that does not matter. But it is good to be the reader of your piece as well as the writer. The theme of a creative work is the underlying message of that work.

Note: War is a word – at best, a topic. 'War proves nothing' is a theme.
Note: Love is a word – at best, a topic. 'It is better to have loved and lost than never to have loved at all' is a theme.

The purpose of theme:

1. To cause the reader to reflect upon the significance of a creative work.
2. To 'bind', or unify, a given piece of writing; to give that writing integrity or unity of design. (*Integrity* comes from Latin *integritas*, meaning 'intact', or 'whole'.)

How do we insert clues as to theme in our writing? Annie Dillard gives some suggestions:

> In most cases the writer of thoughtful literary fiction … simply cannot refrain from waving little flags … . He makes liberal use of epigraphs which plainly raise the intellectual issues at hand. He gives his work a mystifying title … . He slips other clues into the text with a syringe or with a sledgehammer. (Dillard, 1982: 160)

Creating Theme

1. We can write a piece to a chosen theme: 'Be true to yourself'.
2. We can repeat a significant word or phrase (a 'trope') throughout a narrative that will ultimately be 'interpreted out' (recognized) as carrying the thematic message.
3. We might use a significant lesser anecdote or narrative within our major narrative to emphasize the same message as the major narrative, thus creating a 'standout' thematic idea.
4. Most importantly, we might not be aware or conscious initially that our narratives or poems even have a theme, after writing a first draft. After reflection we go back and, in a redrafting, enrich, increase or complicate the role of one of the characters or the plot to develop a theme. A first attempt at a simple crime story might become 'theme

enriched' so that when the character is caught, found out or confesses (as in Poe's 'Tell Tale Heart' 1983: 3–4) the theme that 'crime doesn't pay' or 'the truth will come to light' emerges.

> **HIDDEN NARRATIVE EXERCISE**
>
> Write a paragraph of 100–200 words that begins with the freewrite from this chapter. Embed a theme or hidden narrative in the paragraph so that a reader might be able to describe what it is about on the surface (the 'triggering' subject) and also speculate what it is 'really' about underneath.

Romance, Thrillers, True Crime and Other Genre Fiction

What if we are not after gravitas or literary awards or deeper meanings or Nobel Prizes, and what if we simply want a good plot-driven story that gets readers to turn pages as fast as they can?

The tools we use to create narrative flow are the same, but we have to use them in a more conscious, planned way.

Mysteries, thrillers and romances depend on a triggering and an underlying plot that is careful and well crafted. If all the writer's tools in this book are put to use to write a good romance, the results should be fantastic. Readers of genre fiction want to be catapulted into an exciting alternate reality. If there's a deeper theme to the story, fine, but the narrative movement and what happens to the characters is paramount. Planning and writing a mystery novel, for example, require us to write two plots: one, the surface plot, and one hidden. We are writing to deceive and cannot say what really happened (until the end). We know that X is the murderer, but we have to pretend that Y is, and deceive and misdirect our readers until the twist at the end, when all is revealed. In the classic romance, we know that A and B will live happily ever after, but at first they have to hate each other or misunderstand each other's character and actions. This tension or complication, the conflict, is fundamental. Even in literary fiction and poetry, the writer has to wait until the end for denouement (the unravelling of the complicated knot).

This can be achieved in two ways. We either plan out the stories and then write the surface plot, slowly revealing the underlying plot with clues and implications, or we set out like the reader, not knowing who the murderer is, or how the lovers will work out their differences, and discover them as we write. There is no 'right' way to create any work, but there are easier roads and much, much harder ones.

PAUL

I recommend the first careful planning way, although I have always foolishly sweated through the second, not knowing myself who the murderer is. The advantage of the second method is that we are in the eyes of the reader and that the mystery will be real. The disadvantage is that we then have to go back and rewrite the story when we find out, so we can plant clues and misdirect. But at least the journey is genuine. I write to find out something, and it is as surprising to me as it is for the reader when I do.

The way any narrative moves depends on all of the elements discussed in previous chapters. The journey, or the plot, is what we have at the end when we look back at the map and understand the territory we've just travelled. Themes, character, voice, positioning and tense are all part of the big, slow unfolding of the narrative journey. We can plan our journey in great detail, making sure that all the ends tie up, aware of exactly what lies beneath and what rolls by on the surface. Or we can just set out with a compass and a collection of tools and strategies, and trust that by the end, even though we may have taken some detours, we reach the destination we anticipated.

Oh, and of course, even with carefully planned journeys, one should always allow for deviations from the route and expect the unexpected along the way.

FURTHER READING AND RELEVANT EXAMPLES

Freud's *The Interpretation of Dreams* is always a good place to start to explore the mechanisms and language of repression.

Joseph Campbell's *Hero of a Thousand Faces* is a must for those who want to understand the hero's journey and the archetypal formulae that work in fiction and the epic poem as well as in film.

10
Innovations

> **Freewrite #10**
>
> *I take flight shortly thereafter ...*

In a (fictional) autobiography of his own life, J. M. Coetzee describes his vision of his future writing career:

> What he would write if he could ... would be something darker, something that, once it began to flow from his pen, would spread across the page out of control, like spilt ink. Like spilt ink, like shadows racing across the face of still water, like lightning crackling across the sky. (Coetzee, 1997: 140)

PAUL

In my last year of high school, my English teacher, Miss Botha (we never knew her first name then), inspired a whole generation of boys (I went to an all-male school) to write. I remember the exact moment I was inspired to become a writer. She asked us to read a passage from James Joyce's Portrait of the Artist as a Young Man, *where the protagonist is walking on the beach. He is about to become a priest and take his vows, but he sees a woman swimming in the sea and walking onto the beach. Her beauty is a vision that inspires him to leave the Church and to become a writer, to become, in his words, a 'priest of the imagination'. I too decided then and there to become a priest of the imagination, to explore new worlds, to experiment, to dare to dream, to write.*

Every so often, a new book explodes on the scene that takes everyone by surprise. It may have an innovative title, a theme that's quirky, or it may be crafted with such unique skill that regardless of the story, readers are mesmerized. And so of course, once in a while a writer's dream of being a literary inventor, of coming up with something that is both unique and universal and unexpected, comes true. Any creative mind will be inspired to push boundaries, to find new ways of expressing age-old themes and to connect to the readers of a particular point in history – the present. There are poets who push the very boundaries of language by making words do things we don't expect them to, and there are non-fiction writers who employ techniques that have readers glued to their pages as if they were reading a high-stakes thriller; and in fiction, sometimes a new approach or new style or thought changes the whole lay of the literary landscape.

This final chapter takes us to the places where we can consider that the only limits are the ones we impose, and where we might find the true beginnings of who we can be as makers and creators of new worlds and ways of seeing those.

The Postmodern Mind

Postmodernism is a term that has been abused and overused so much so that it has become a cliché. We live in a postmodern era. Whatever we write now is postmodern. The term comes from Ihab Hassan's book *The Post Modern Turn*, an exploration of the historical rejection of Modernism, which (to simplify) was a rejection of Realism, which itself was a rejection of Romanticism, and so on. The literary sweep from Realism (Victorian era) to Modernism (early twentieth century) to Postmodernism (from the 1960s on) has meant that surely we are in for another rejection now of Postmodernism. Post-postmodernism? But the term *postmodern* has stalled any further definitions. It has defeated us. Or perhaps it has stuck because we like the inherent absurdity of the contradiction. If modern is the present, postmodern is the future. There can be nothing after it.

At its heart, postmodernism acknowledges that language does not have a one-on-one simple relation to the world it describes. Whereas realist writing assumes that what is described is what is out there, modernism problematizes this, demonstrating that whatever is out there can only be apprehended subjectively. Postmodernism goes further and declares that there is no 'out there' at all, that our 'reality' (always in quotes!) is constructed through language, and we can only refer to a self-enclosed language system of signs.

The gift of postmodernism is that as far as writing is concerned, it allows us to play. The characteristics of what we call 'postmodern writing' are irony, playfulness, black humour, word play, linguistic gymnastics. Postmodernism parodies older forms, expresses itself in pastiche, writes on top of other forms, delights in contradiction, juxtaposition and exposure of the mechanisms of literary production. Contemporary creative writing, then, is less and less about objective reality and more and more about its own creative processes.

This is a relief. As writers we're liberated into the new, the never done before. We can find more ways to play with words. We can employ postmodern frameworks to innovate and be refreshingly new.

Palimpsest

A palimpsest is a piece of writing or artwork written or painted on top of another so that we can see the previous artwork behind it. In the 1960s, the word *palimpsest* began to be used as a metaphor for the way language writes the author, and in order to undermine the notion of the 'author' as originator or creator of the text. For Kristeva, 'any text is constructed of a mosaic of quotations; any text is the absorption and transformation of another' (1986).

Of course, all writing takes place in the presence of other writings – and palimpsests acknowledge this, undermining the idea that any author is the sole creator or source of his or her work. Matthew Lewis, author of *The Monk* (1796), puts it neatly: '[T]he best ideas are borrowed from other poets, though possibly you are unconscious of the theft yourself' (2009, 7).

T. S. Eliot, both writer and critic, suggests that such conscious intertextuality and the creation of palimpsests are vital tools for a serious writer's craft. Far from being unconscious or unintentional, he argues in 'Tradition and the Individual Talent' that poets need to consciously immerse themselves in the history of poetry in order to be able to write on top of the great tradition of letters that has preceded them: 'No poet, no artist of any art, has his complete meaning alone. His significance, his appreciation is the appreciation of his relation to the dead poets and artists' (1965: 5–6).

PAUL

Probably the best example of intertextuality I can find is Salinger's Catcher in the Rye, *the 1950s novel that heralded teen literature. In the beginning of the book, the narrator Holden Caulfield tells us he is going to tell his story, but warns us that he is not going to tell us his 'whole goddam autobiography' or any of that 'David Copperfield kind of crap'. The allusion* is to Charles Dickens's fictional autobiography of the same name. *But what makes this more than an allusion and more a palimpsest is that the more we read, the more we see that* Catcher in the Rye *is written 'on top of'* David Copperfield, *and readers need the Dickens novel to make sense of the Salinger one. For example, the character David Copperfield was born with a caul over his head, a natural protective covering and, according to tradition, a symbol of good luck. The main protagonist of* Catcher in the Rye *wears a red cap throughout the novel as protection and for luck. And if we do not get the intertextual connection, Salinger makes it more obvious by naming his main protagonist 'Holden Caulfield.'*

I often make allusions in my stories to other works of art. In my short story 'Promise Me This', I refer to the 'bolgie' of our society. This refers to Dante's layers of hell in The Inferno. *But it is (I hope) more than just a smarmy reference to show off my literary knowledge. I wanted when I wrote that to connect my story and the layers of deceit of our society to the layers of hell in Dante's poem so that the two would resonate off each other (Williams 2012: 212).*

> **UPCYCLING AND RECYCLING IDEAS EXERCISE**
>
> Choose a well-loved novel or poem or character or all of those and write a 150-word passage alluding to any element in that novel or poem or about that character. Include a line from the piece in your title, use the name of a character, or an event, or an object (like Caulfield's red cap). Weave allusions into the passage from that story/poem until they begin to 'need' each other in order to exist.

Bowerbirding, Bricolage and Plagiarism

Like all inventors, we like to believe we're able to produce something completely new, something never seen before. But the honest truth is, even as we produce the latest innovation, we are all takers of one kind or another, and what we as writers most frequently pilfer is other writing. Literature is our raw material. We consciously or unconsciously feed off other writers, observe, try out techniques and steal plots (because, of course, there are apparently only two).

Bowerbirding is a narrative technique that acknowledges how we pick out the things we need for our narratives from a wide variety of sources, 'like a bowerbird that picks out the blue things and leaves all the other colours' (Brady, 2000); *bricolage*, 'a pieced together, close-knit set of practices' (Stewart, 2001), refers to the sampling and internalization of all these things, whether they are theories, other books, real stories – anything, really, under the sun.

So, this is the game writers play. We will always be there, taking on both the conscious and unconscious task of creating intertextual palimpsests, scraping off and writing on top of the old, innovating, modifying past texts and allowing readers to play alongside us, in the game of dusting off words and finding others underneath. Although we may not be the originators of all the meaning that we end up creating, we are constantly in dialogue with the past and the future. Let the game continue!

Polyphonic Voice

In chapter 3, we looked at voice. But we looked at voice in the singular. In a postmodern context, voice is plural. And that's the nature of the world we live in. We're immersed daily in clashing voices and narratives. Our whole lives revolve around different texts in different mediums: we might watch a political debate on TV, be engaged simultaneously in reading a string of contradictory Twitter feeds at the bottom of the screen and text a friend who isn't feeling well about how mad the world is.

Polyphony is everywhere. And it's been around a while. Mikhail Bakhtin borrowed the phrase from a musical concept, referring to the diversity of voices in Dostoyevsky's novels. But recently, there has been a resurgence of novels of this type that play with simultaneity, contradiction and the empty space between voices, echoing our postmodern, multitasking reading practice.

The word *polyphonic* is a musical term, referring to simultaneous lines of independent melody making a whole. Most music is polyphonic, but the term has come to mean a complex interweaving of melodies associated with counterpoint, for example Bach's fugues, where each part is written against the other, intertwining, playing off the main melody line, sometimes playing it in reverse, harmonizing at opportune moments.

According to David Lodge, a polyphonic novel is a 'novel in which a variety of conflicting ideological positions are given a voice and set in play both between and within individual speaking subjects, without being placed and judged by an authoritative authorial voice' (1990: 86).

In a monological novel, readers get comfortable with a particular point of view and narrative voice. In polyphonic novels, however, voices interact, and to make things exciting, they often mitigate against each other.

Writers (and readers) are now embracing simultaneity, contradiction, the empty space between voices, cacophony and multimedia intrusions into the genre. The polyphonous novel reflects new technology, plays with it, rails against it. Voice is no longer a metaphor. Form, format, genre, multimedia have extended its meaning to encompass more than just the author's style or persona. The postmodern polyphonic novel allows a multitasking operation, which deliberately flouts authorial control or linguistic stability, celebrating discord and irruption of any monologic voice.

SHELLEY

Lights Over Emerald Creek *relies on the reader going to look up elements that inspired the story. At the back of the book, I give a description of real events, such as the well-documented but still unexplained phenomenon of the Hessdalen lights in Norway, cymatics and the bizarre hexagonal storm on Saturn's north pole captured by the Cassini craft and on NASA's website, all of which play a role in the novel. One reader wrote in a review: 'If I could give the author 5 stars for the research and info I learned from the book, I would have. Although it was a quick read, I took longer because I Googled everything. If you don't want to read the book, buy it for the info, which what the book is based on is true. It was well worth reading for that knowledge alone. I think the author should write a true story about that. It is fascinating!' (https://www.goodreads.com/book/show/20430396-lights-over-emerald-creek).*

I don't know what a 'true story' would look like, but I am thinking about it!

As writers writing in a digital postmodern, polyphonous age, the page is no longer our only text-bearer. New technologies are providing previously unimaginable arenas for our narratives. Nigel Krauth, in his book *Creative Writing and the Radical*, argues for the novel of the future that embraces new technology and its multiple discourses in terms of form and interactivity (2016). A multigraphic novel will mimic our multitasking postmodern habits as we listen, search, engage in side narratives, watch visual text and follow seemingly contradictory strands of discourses all at once. Competing voices can be added to texts, with a visual component, interactive and live links (for e-books) and audio soundtrack. Even in a standard print text, such disruptive voices can be explored in a variety of ways, signalled by font changes, format differences and intrusion of other genres.

Here is a sample from a first-year creative writing student, Lachlan Haycock's 'Edge', which uses experimental typography and multiple discourses in order to explore bipolar affective disorder:

> The man would have been content to remain there slumped, but scrambled to right himself after tendrils of adrenal liquid began to leak through his veins. It was happening. He was feeling the beginnings of that *urge* emerging from within.
>   *haven't slept*   *feeling hot*
>   *stricken, neighbours keeping me up all night*
>
> He pushed up with lanky arms and grabbed at the child, held him to his side.
> He knew it. It was happening.
> A Red Sea of pedestrians parted before him; the man lurched at the opportunity (bangshickshick). He rubbed at crimson-edged eyes and pushed back his fringe in a single motion, then scrambled into the gap before it was filled. The fabric of his shirt rippled and the air around his ears funnelled as a breeze swept through. The crowd in front of him slowed as cars were given the green light. But he just pushed ahead through, made it to the curb and kept going, leaping between buses. Squealing brakes, honking horns.
>   *missing buttons...must remember to fix*

And here is a third-year student's story, Tracey White's 'Blackbird', a complex palimpsest where one story of slavery and oppression is overlain with another, an almost illegible embedded ghost story:

> *I poke deeper, among the meagre stuffing, finding more tightly packed scrolls of dry cane leaf.*
>
> Didn't we first flee the city?
>   As soon as we could we made our move, blind then to the refuge that bleak existence gave us; with a stolen car and a tank of bio we left.
>   For what?
>   The chance to find that whispered path to freedom, together, to the islands of the north?
>   So very in love.
>   And so naïve.   *Didn't we flee the city,*
>   'Come over here,' you'd say, one hand on the wheel, elbow on the window, glancing at me sideways; your look humid with mirth. I slid across the bench-seat to press against you, tucked under your wing; and we rode through rain that fell for days in warm sheets over the cane; hearts and wipers beating. *above?*
>   When we met the sewer line, we knew we'd found trouble.
>   After the car spluttered to a halt we tracked on foot, through the maze of harvest roads, north we hoped, ever north, knowing the mills lay inland; the waste of millions pumped through a radiating network of giant, impassable veins to feed them. | *Bleak our discontent, and*

Polyphonic novels reflect our multitasking functions, mirroring our fragmented and schizophrenic (another metaphor) new century.

1
Blaberus craniifer
Death-head cockroach

> The death-head cockroach or *Blaberus craniifer* is marked with a dark spot on its thorax, which, with a stretch of the imagination, looks like a skull. It will eat anything, even faeces, to satisfy its hunger. It has wings, but is incapable of flight, and chooses rather to confront its enemies by emitting a repulsive odour. It is most commonly found in so-called Third World countries, and because of its markings is often the victim of negative projections.

You're driving down a red dirt road in the middle of South Africa, having turned off at the intersection of nowhere and nowhere. You're lost. You're late for a meeting. The aircon in the rental car doesn't work, and you're wearing a European suit. You should stop and ask for directions, but you're male, genetically programmed never to ask for directions.

Three men stand in the road. One brandishes a panga—a machete. One points the barrel of an AK-47 at your face. The middle one holds up the open palm of his hand and bangs on the bonnet. You stop the car.

'Where you going, *umlungu*?'[1]

'Open up here, sharp sharp, man.'

Your blood runs cold.

No, no, no. Your blood does not bloody run cold. Only the blood of ectothermic creatures, like frogs, fish, geckos, crocodiles, chameleons, snakes, spiders, centipedes and cockroaches, runs cold. Your blood

---

1 *Umlungu*. Zulu (n). Derogatory. White man. Origin: white foam on the beach, i.e. white scum.

What is fundamental about modern polyphonic novels is that the author does not place his or her own narrative voice between the character and the reader. The text appears as an interaction of distinct perspectives or ideologies borne by the different characters. The characters are able to speak for themselves, even against the author – it is as if the author speaks directly through the text. The role of the author is fundamentally changed because the author can no longer monopolize the power to mean.

Any written narrative is a construct, and it's possible that the modern polyphonic novel is a more authentic representation of the ways we construct and negotiate our modern narrative self in the world.

PAUL

Cokcraco *is a polyphonic novel. At first I tried to use one voice, but felt that I needed to loosen my grip of authority on the text and allow others to speak too and contradict myself. No longer am I the Nabokovian 'absolute dictator' over my characters, but a conductor of rebellious voices, dangerous though that may be. Polyphony may easily become cacophony, but then I have to trust in the reader's skills in the modern art of multitasking.*

OVERTHROW THE DICTATOR EXERCISE

Write a passage (100–200 words). Add a contradictory voice to it. Interweave or simply juxtapose voices in separate paragraphs. Disturb the monologue. Overthrow the dictator. Use counter-voices to disrupt.

Or:

Imagine your text as an e-book. Add gifs, images, sound, links and feeds to it. Celebrate the multiplicity of voices that we have at our fingertips these days to mirror a modern (post) experience of reading texts.

The Composite Novel

The composite novel blurs the distinction between the short story and the novel. A composite novel is a collection of short stories that connects in theme or has the same characters, as well as a novel with a set of discrete chapters that loosely converge.

PAUL

I have been writing steadily about my relationship with my father and published several short stories that deal with his death, his secret affairs, his attempt to apprentice me as a magician. Each story is complete in itself, but when I combine them and present them as a 'novel', a pattern emerges, a narrative structure that fits like a jigsaw puzzle. I add a few tweaks – connecting characters and events in each story, and I have a composite novel. Also, I am attempting a novel about the Middle East. I cannot find the right angle, and it feels tedious to write a long narrative that trails my arduous journey from beginning to end, so I instead write scenes, or short stories, one about my job interview, another about my students, another from the point of view of a friend of mine. And at a certain point, a fragmentary novel takes shape that can be pieced together in terms of theme, characters, plot.

> **FRAGMENTS EXERCISE**
>
> Put two of your short stories together and see how they read next to each other. Are there any common themes or characters? Plant a character from one story in another as a side character. Or a theme. Play with the stories. If you change the order, do they read differently?

Borrowings: Ergodic Texts

Ergodic texts are elements of a new genre that plays with forms and whose format and structure is unconventional and interacts with electronic media. Espen J. Aarseth coined the phrase in his book *Cybertext – Perspectives on Ergodic Literature* (1997). The genre breaks free of the idea that a text is always print based or that it is self-enclosed. A pile of rain-sodden newspapers could be an ergodic text; so could a series of text messages or an interaction between reader and writer via Twitter. Ergodic literature could include the readers' responses to the text received. Ergodic forms of textuality situate the writer-reader in the same space and connect the digital and the textual.

Paul's novel *Cokcraco* contains footnotes (borrowed from the academic essay convention), box inserts as used in textbooks, different fonts, intrusive voices, travel guides, poems and epigraphs, interrupting the narrative. The layout of the page is also subverted, using poetic form, concrete poetry and white space to tell the story. Ergodic literature makes readers work hard and does not allow them to slip through the squiggly lines into a single meaning.

Ergodic literature challenges readers to make sense of a text. It reveals the ways in which we make meaning of the many contradictions in the realities that bombard us in everyday life. It even challenges the way we move our eyes across the page, the way we turn pages. For example, we read Internet newsfeeds, Facebook pages and text in a multitasking way that would confuse and perplex nineteenth-century readers.

PAUL

My mother, who is in her late eighties and is not adept at modern technology, cannot read a Facebook page and keeps asking me, 'Where am I supposed to look? The pictures and writing keep changing!'

> **INTERRUPTED NARRATIVE EXERCISE**
>
> Write a series of passages that experiment with form. Play with the placement of words on a page and change formatting, style and fonts. Use inserts from other texts. Imitate the way we read these days.

Antinomacy: Reverse Chronology

Who says that stories have to be told forwards? Martin Amis's *Time's Arrow* (1991), for example, is a story that begins with a Nazi war criminal's death and reverses all the way back to his birth. Kurt Vonnegut's *Slaughterhouse 5* (1969) includes a passage where World War II bombings are told backwards. Since Einstein's theory on the relativity of space and time, we have regarded time as fluid, and reversible. Our writing does not need to be imprisoned in a forward linear time. Our minds don't work that way anyway, so it makes sense to experiment with the idea of time in a narrative. Play with flashbacks, flash forwards, sequence.

For example:

> He unswallowed
> chewed for long minutes
> and then carefully
> removed the baby
> potato from his mouth
> with a fork

He placed it on the plate
uncut it, removed
the hot melted butter
with a knife
and watched
as the potato grew
hotter and hotter
He sucked in air from his mouth to heat it
After waiting awhile, he stabbed
the potato
with a fork
and placed it in the oven
where he watched it harden and cool.
His stomach
Rumbled
Finally, he picked it up with his fingers
and under the tap
brushed dirt onto it.
Then he walked
backwards
out into the garden
and carefully buried it
in the red earth
And smoothed
the ground over it.

> **TURNING BACK TIME EXERCISE**
>
> Write a piece backwards. This can be a piece that literally follows a narrative from end to beginning (the classic plot being an old person who gets younger until he or she becomes a baby and disappears). Or the sections can be reversed. If the piece is a poem, even the words can be reversed to create new meaning.

Ecriture Feminine: Writing the Body

Hélène Cixous, the twentieth-century French feminist writer, argues that women should strive to avoid the patriarchal detached 'objective' writing of the mainstream and attempt to 'write the body': 'Woman must write her self: must write about women and bring women to writing, from which they have been driven away as violently as from their bodies' (Cixous, 1976: 875).

Writers often think that writing comes from their thinking selves, their imaginations, their abstract ideas, and that writing is the act of embodying these ideas. But that is a very Platonic way of thinking. What if it were the other way around, if our writing was a physical act like excreting sweat or blood? Declaring our bodies. Both male and female writers can benefit from the idea of writing about the physicality of self.

Example:

> My head aches as I write this. My neck is out. I should never have done those cartwheels on the beach yesterday. I swear I have sprained my hand. Yet I could not stop. I needed that exuberance of tumbling upside down over and over, round and round, the blood rushing to my head, going so dizzy I could not stand straight, as if I were on a small spinning world whose gravity clamped me to the ground. I spat sand. I laughed. The pure joy of being in my body again, as if I had forgotten I had one. A body not just to haul around, but a body that laughed, dizzied me and now aches and shows me how many muscles I do have that I never knew until I started using them.

SHELLEY

My young adult novel Spirit of the Mountain *(2009) explores the idea of anorexia. It includes my own diary entries from a time when I was starving myself from age fourteen to seventeen. I wrote about my body, about food – obsessively. My body was the territory I traversed with my words of derision, self-loathing, desperation and ultimately desire for things to be different. In a sense, my body became the canvas on which I could paint my statement: if millions were starving, and I could do nothing about it, I could at least make sure that if the millions of children could* not eat, *I would* not eat. *Being a fat white girl in South Africa was not okay by me.*

Example:

> Her head fell against the door and she dozed off, listening to the hum of the engine. Slowly, through watery dreams, the thin body of the ancient man appeared. Before her eyes he grew younger and younger, until he was just a child ... she knew she should give the strange withered child something to eat. He had not eaten for 5000

years and she could feel his hunger inside her own stomach. She brought a spoon of porridge to his shrivelled lips, but as she did so her own hunger grew so strong that she stopped the spoon in mid-air. (Davidow, 2009: 25)

> **ALIENS AND ANGELS EXERCISE**
>
> Write a passage (100–150 words, poetry or prose) to an alien, an angel or any imaginary non-sentient being who does not know what it is like to be human and to live in a physical body with five senses. Describe to the visitor how it feels to be in a body. Describe the aches and pains, the pleasures, the sensations of touch, smell, taste, hearing, sight, the phenomenon of being alive. Declare physicality.

Magic Realism

We can probably all think of strange dreams we've had where the impossible happened and we accepted those happenings without questioning their strangeness.

SHELLEY

When I was a teenager, I dreamt I was in an art class, and the teacher opened a drawer in a cupboard. I looked into the drawer and saw an amazing sight: a beautiful turquoise-green sea was breaking onto a golden shore in the drawer. I was above it, looking in, loving the colours and the small breaking waves. 'Just dip your brush into the colour of Sprite,' said the teacher, and without thinking anything was strange, I put my brush into the greenest part of the sea, excited about the colour. I had no sense that there was anything strange at all about what I was doing.

This is essentially what magic realism is – a narrative technique that blurs the distinction between fantasy and reality, characterized by an acceptance on the part of the narrator and reader of the magic as real, of the extraordinary as ordinary. The effect this has is to view magic, fantastic events as natural. Gabriel García Márquez is the name that springs to mind first when we speak of magic realism, for example his story where a moth-eaten angel falls to earth and is kept like a mangy pet in a chicken cage, or the one with a community who do not have to sleep at night so can work double the hours without ever getting tired. But the roots of this genre go back much further, to Kafka's *Metamorphosis* and before.

When asked how he created this new form of writing, Márquez said, 'My most important problem was destroying the lines of demarcation that separates [sic] what seems real from what seems fantastic' (Kelby, 2009).

When writing magic realism, it's important not to confuse it with fantasy.

In fantasy, a world is consistent. If people fly and are not surprised by it, it is a consistency in that world. But magic realism is incongruent, and things happen without an explanation. Magical realism sets magical events in realistic contexts, thus requiring us to question what is 'real'. Also, magic realism often has the quality of gritty realism, so a flying carpet would be perhaps a bit worn, difficult to stay on top of, might undulate in the wind and crumple when the wind dropped; a fantastic flying carpet would take a protagonist, Aladdin-like, without question of wind or weather, to his destination.

Example:

> He found her washed up on the beach just before the sun rose. Her long hair had tangled itself around bits of coral. Her tail bled near the end, where a blade from some speedboat had cut into her. As he approached the mermaid, she beat the hard sand with her tail and pulled herself along the shoreline and cried, saying, 'Go away, go away!'

WASHED UP ON THE BEACH EXERCISE

Write realistically (poetry or prose) about a magical event, using realistic techniques. The teller of the event should not express surprise at the magical phenomenon, which happens without explanation or reason.

Creative Nonfiction

What about blurring the boundaries between fact and fiction consciously in a work? Creative nonfiction does just this, in nice contradiction. Truman Capote in 1953 coined the term *non-fiction novel*, a 'narrative form that employed all the techniques of fictional art but was nevertheless immaculately factual' (Capote in Plimpton, 1966).

PAUL

I was asked to write the story of an Iraqi man whose daughter was killed in a roadside bomb. I interviewed him and took notes, which looked like this:

- In hospital my son was very good. My uncle stayed by his side every day and we talked of things. I said, Rasheed, don't pick the what-do-you-call-them?
- Scabs.
- Don't pick the scabs. They healed very quickly, his head OK. His arm broken. Fingers. How we heal, it's a miracle, said his uncle, a miracle.

The final product, after editing, smoothing out grammatical errors and using narrative techniques, 'inventing' dialogue, looked like this:

He went to the hospital every night for three months. His uncle was a faithful friend, sat by his son's bedside, and they talked, to while away the night hours.

The wounds began to heal. He picked shrapnel out of his own flesh for months. His son was now covered in deep purple scabs. Don't pick at them Mohammed. Don't pick. They're itchy because they're healing.

'It's a miracle, this healing,' said his uncle. 'A miracle'. (Williams, 2012: 'Green Island')

The point is that we have to invent, add, rearrange, 'fictionalize' events to give an emotional truth rather than a literal one, because memory is deceptive, and stories, unlike raw life, are shaped by narrative form. But there is still accountability. The Iraqi man read over and approved my story as accurate, even though it was not strictly 'true'.

SHELLEY

I have to say that writing literary non-fiction has been an unexpectedly wonderful journey. It's sort of confining, in that the events are already set out, and real life is often more subtle or dramatic than the events we construct carefully in a fictional narrative. But working with historical events and reimagining the things no one could possibly actually know has been a humbling and revealing experience. In Whisperings in the Blood, *I immersed myself in the voices of people (my grandmother and grandfather) living in the United States and South Africa in the 1930s by reading their letters, and as a result their characters emerged for me as alive and present as if I had known them. It was the closest experience to time travel I could ever have imagined.*

Historiographic Metafiction

We no longer write 'history' or autobiography or biography. Our readers are smart enough to know that whatever 'factual history' that is written is constructed, shaped (fictionalized). The best we can do is to acknowledge that we are subjectively shaping, interpreting or manipulating facts to create story. Here is the disclaimer at the beginning of Paul's memoir, in which he admits that he has had great difficulty presenting his life story as 'fact' or as autobiography or as history.

DISCLAIMER from *Soldier Blue*:

Although this is a memoir and strives to give a 'true' account of the narrator's life, certain events, characters, and characters' names have been changed/ blended together to protect identities, and to telescope history into manageable proportions. As Azar Nafisi says in her Author's Note to *Reading Lolita in Tehran*, 'the facts in this story are true insofar as all memories are true'; that is, all history is fictionalised, second-hand, and transmuted by the act of writing into the language of myth, dream and metaphor. (Williams, 2008: 4)

Historiographic metafiction is a genre that acknowledges such subjectivity and invites the reader into the fiction-making process of writing history.

PAUL

I could have written my novel like this:

They [my parents] arrived in Rhodesia, with a pram full of saucepans, a few shillings jangling in their pockets and an optimistic trust in a benevolent universe, that things would somehow work out.

My first memory is a stark image of the white bars of my cot, a square, mauve wallpapered room. ... I waved goodbye to my mother every morning as she guiltily drove off to work.

The problem I faced in recounting 'the truth' in my memoir was that my initial research methodology (naively dredging up memories and writing them down as accurately as possible) did not yield any fruitful results. Not only were my memories unreliable, constructed and false; they were also trivial. All I could do, then, was to record these memories in ways that revealed their unreliability and that exposed them as fictional constructs. So instead I wrote my memoir like this:

> They [my parents] arrived in Rhodesia, the story goes, with a pram full of saucepans, a few shillings jangling in their pockets, and an optimistic trust in a benevolent universe, that things would somehow work out. That's how they tell it, anyhow.
>
> My first memory apparently is a stark image of the white bars of my cot, a square, mauve wallpapered room. … I am also told that I waved goodbye to my mother every morning as she guiltily drove off to work. (Williams, 2008: 7)

The difference? I destabilize 'history' and invite the reader to see the making of history.

SHAPING HISTORY EXERCISE

Write a creative account (200 words) of an actual event, personal or historical. Use characters that are familiar and events that actually happened, but use a modern point of view that is informed by living here and now, to comment on and frame the narrative.

Conclusion: Pushing the Boundaries

PAUL

I first became aware of what Robert Scholes calls the 'spectrum' of truth writing when I read his excellent introduction to fiction (The Elements of Fiction, 1968) where he points out that there is not much difference between fact *(Latin:* facere *– 'to make or do') and* fiction *(Latin:* fingere *– 'to make or shape'). Nor is there much difference between* story *(histoire) and* history *(histoire). Scholes clearly imagined a spectrum of writing which looked like this:*

  History
      Journalism
           Autobiography
                 Creative Nonfiction
                      Memoir
                         Realism
                             Romanticism
                                 Fantasy

> Taking these two extremes [fact and fiction] as the opposite ends of a whole spectrum of fictional possibilities, between the infrared of pure history and the ultraviolet of pure imagination, we can distinguish many shades of coloration. But all are fragments of the white radiance of truth, which is present in both history books and fairy tales, but only partly present in each – fragmented by the prism of fiction, without which we should not be able to see it at all. (Scholes, 1968: 4)

Scholes advocates for the primacy of fiction as the way of making sense of experience. It is not fact or fiction, or truth versus lies, or myth versus reality: everything we think or do is mediated with words, through language, through the story-telling devices in our brains.

> Fact, in order to survive, must become fiction. A thing done has no real existence once it has been done. It may have consequences, and there may be many records that point to its former existence, but once it is done, its existence is finished. A thing made (such as a fiction), on the other hand, exists until it is decayed or destroyed. (Scholes 1968: 4)

All the playing with words we have done up until this point in the book can be applied to poetry, fiction, non-fiction or memoir, or personal essay. The divide between these forms that we have come to call by so many different names is more tenuous than we think, and perhaps doesn't even exist at all. We are making worlds with our words, and whether the images have their roots in events we know happened or in the recesses of overactive imaginations (fed unconsciously by our experiences perhaps), the results are always the same: we write a realm into existence, and a reader enters.

The point is that whatever we are writing, the genre and the medium are only the means. In scientific writing, factual report writing and journalism, we are using words to portray truth. In fantasy, magic realism and science fiction, we are using words to portray truth. Truth resides nowhere and everywhere, and ultimately exists when a reader finds resonance with our writing, when our thoughts are wrapped in the words and sentences that come closest to representing the essence of our complex, nebulous and often fleeting world of ideas.

INNOVATIVE POETRY, FICTION AND OTHER RELEVANT EXAMPLES TO EXPLODE THE MIND

Reading James Joyce's *Portrait of the Artist as a Young Man* takes the reader on a journey into what can be possible in terms of stream of consciousness. If you can handle it, then move on to *Ulysses* and *Finnegans Wake*.

T. S. Eliot's *The Wasteland* is an exercise in intertextuality, a collection of broken fragments.

J. D. Salinger's *The Catcher in the Rye* is worth reading as a palimpsest.

Martin Amis's *Time's Arrow* will make you start thinking backwards, even dreaming backwards.

Kurt Vonnegut's *Slaughterhouse Five* will do your mind in on various levels.

For Ecriture Feminine, read A. S. Byatt's *Little Black Book of Stories*, particularly 'Body Art', and for the adventurous, read the transgressive Kathy Acker.

In order to experience magic realism, read Kafka's *The Metamorphosis*, *The Trial* or any of his short stories, such as 'The Hunger Artist'. Marquez's classic *One Hundred Years of Solitude* is a prime example of how he blends fantasy and realism so seamlessly that we do not know where one begins and one ends.

Appendix

Self and Peer Review Editing Template for Fiction and Narrative Non-fiction

Name _____

1. **Moving through Time and Space: Narrative Flow and Plot Logic Overview.** Does the narrative hold together and is it logical how events unfold, or is there anything confusing? Is the narrative appropriate for the target audience? Is there enough of a conflict to keep a reader reading?

   COMMENTS:

2. **Voice, Word Choice, Sentences.** Does the vocabulary choice and sentence structure (short sentences, long sentences) support the narrative? Does the 'voice' of the writer emerge as distinctive? Is there a sound/rhythm to the voice? Do metaphors (extended or otherwise) or symbolism appear as part of the creation of that distinctive voice? Are words chosen with care, or are there several aspects of lazy writing/overwriting that could be addressed to make the piece stronger? Are there spaces or silences (elision) that are effective?

   COMMENTS:

3. **Those Who Speak: The Setting, Character and Dialogue and Angling for a View.** Do the settings support/reflect underlying

themes? Is there foreshadowing? Does the dialogue serve to reveal the characters and their relationships and to move the plot along? Is the point of view and use of tense appropriate to the subject?

COMMENTS:

4. **Creativity/Innovation/Research.** Is there something new, something innovative about the piece that pushes boundaries – a structural innovation, evidence of research or something uniquely creative about the voice or style? Do words work, perhaps in unexpected ways? What 'hooks' the reader?

COMMENTS:

5. **Spelling, Grammar, Punctuation and Paragraphing.** Ensure that everything is as clean as possible. Here are common errors that sometimes go undetected when reading our own writing: *its, it's, your, you're, their, there, they're, weather, whether.* Check these words to ensure correct usage.

Sample Rubric for Fiction or Narrative Non-fiction

Emerging 1–4   Competent 5–8   Sophisticated 9–10

	COMMENTS
Moving through Time and Space This mark reflects an evaluation of how the narrative holds together and how overall plot logic unfolds, taking into account the use of conflict to hook readers and whether the piece is a good fit for its target audience.	/10
Words, Sentences and Voice This mark reflects an assessment of vocabulary choice and 'voice' of the writer. Consideration is given to the use of metaphors and symbolism as well as whether the author is conscious of aspects of unintentional overwriting or lazy writing. It considers whether aspects of elision and silence are used effectively.	/10

Those Who Speak: Characters and Context This mark reflects the way the author uses setting to support/reflect underlying themes; whether dialogue serves to reveal characters and relationships and to move the plot along, as well as how point of view is used.	/10
Creativity/Innovation/Research This mark reflects a response to the new or innovative in the piece – to techniques or ideas that 'hook' the reader.	/10
Structural Elements and Presentation This mark reflects the control of structural elements such as spelling grammar, punctuation, paragraphing and formatting.	/10

Self and Peer Review Editing Template for Poetry

Name _____

1. **Narrative Flow.** Is there flow to the poem and an implicit or explicit unfolding of ideas? (This flow should not be so secret to the writer that it is invisible to a reader. If no one 'gets' it, perhaps 'it' is buried too deep.)

   COMMENTS:

2. **Voice, Word Choice, Sound and Rhythm.** Does the word choice create distinctive voice? Is there a distinctive sound/rhythm? Do metaphors (extended or otherwise) or symbolism appear as part of the distinctive voice? Are words chosen with care? Are line breaks used effectively to affect rhythm and enhance meaning? Are there any aspects of lazy writing/overwriting that could be addressed to make the poem stronger? Are there spaces or silences (elision) that are effective?

   COMMENTS:

3. **Those Who Speak: Point of View.** Is the position of the narrator and tense of the poem supportive of the underlying themes?

   COMMENTS:

4. **Creativity/Innovation/Research.** Is there something new, something innovative about the poem that pushes boundaries, either a structural innovation, evidence of research or something uniquely creative about the voice or style? Do words work, perhaps in unexpected ways? What 'hooks' the reader?

   COMMENTS:

5. **Spelling, Grammar, Punctuation and Paragraphing.** Ensure that everything is as clean as possible. Here are common errors that sometimes go undetected even in poetry, when reading our own writing: *its, it's, your, you're, their, there, they're, weather, whether.* Check these words to ensure correct usage.

Sample Rubric for Poetry

Emerging 1–4   Competent 5–8   Sophisticated 9–10

	COMMENTS
Narrative Flow This mark reflects an assessment of the narrative flow to the poem and the implicit or explicit unfolding of ideas.	/10
Voice, Word Choice, Sound and Rhythm This mark reflects an assessment of a distinctive sound/rhythm. Consideration is given to metaphors (extended or otherwise) or symbolism that may appear as part of the distinctive voice, as well as whether words are chosen with care and whether line breaks are used effectively to effect rhythm and enhance meaning. It considers whether there are aspects of lazy writing/overwriting that could be addressed to make the poem stronger, and whether there are spaces or silences (elision) that are effective.	/10
Point of View This mark reflects a consideration of how the position of the narrator and tense of the poem are supportive of the underlying themes.	/10
Creativity/Innovation/Research This mark reflects a response to the new or innovative in the poem – to techniques or ideas that 'hook' the reader.	/10
Structural Elements and Presentation This mark reflects the control of structural elements such as spelling, grammar and formatting for poetic effect.	/10

References

Adorno, Theodor W. and Shierry Weber Nicholsen. 'Punctuation Marks.' In *Poetry Today* (Summer, 1990): 300–5.

Aarseth, Espen J. *Cybertext – Perspectives on Ergodic Literature*. Baltimore: Johns Hopkins University Press, 1997.

Aldridge, J. W. *Talents and Technicians: Literary Chic and the New Assembly-Line Fiction*. New York: Charles Scribner's and Sons, 1992.

Amis, Martin. *Time's Arrow*. London: Jonathan Cape, 1991.

Archbold, Robin. 'In Praise of Purple Prose – A Maximalist Poem.' https://www.wattpad.com/126240148-basic-human-writes-poetry-stories-in-praise-of (accessed 31 December 2015).

Axelrod, Steven Gould, Camille Roman and Thomas J. Travisano. *The New Anthology of American Poetry: Traditions and Revolutions, Beginnings to 1900*. Rutgers University Press, 2003.

Bail, Murray. *Eucalyptus*. Melbourne: Text Publishing Company, 1999.

Bal, P. Matthijs and Martijn Veltkamp. 'How Does Fiction Reading Influence Empathy? An Experimental Investigation on the Role of Emotional Transportation.' *PLOS ONE* 8, no. 1 (2013).

Bainton, George. *The Art of Authorship*. Whitefish, MT: Kessinger Publishing; Reprint edition. 29 August 2007.

Barthes, Roland. *Writing Degree Zero*. Translated by Annette Lavers and Colin Smith. London: Jonathan Cape Ltd., 1967.

Baudelaire, Charles. 'Mon Coeur mis a nu'. In *Ouevres Completes*. Paris, 1976. Quoted in Fabienne Moore, *Prose Poems of the French Enlightenment: Delimiting Genre*. New York: Ashgate, 2009.

Bianchiotti, Vedette. 'A Study of Gustave Courbet's 'Realism'. *The Journal of Film, Art and Aesthetics*, 20 October 2011.

Brady, Tess. 'A Question of Genre: De-mystifying the Exegesis.' *TEXT* 4, no. 1 (April 2000). http://www.gu.edu.au/school/art/text/ (accessed 26 May 2016).

Braine, John. *How to Write a Novel*. London: Methuen, 2000.

Brautigan, Richard. *A Confederate General from Big Sur*. New York: Houghton Mifflin, 1991.

Brautigan, Richard. *Trout Fishing in America*. New York: Mariner Books, 1967.

Brooks, Gwendolyn. *The Bean Eaters*. New York: Harpers, 1960.

Browning, Robert. 'Porphyria's Lover'. In Arthur Quiller-Couch (ed.), *The Oxford Book of English Verse: 1250–1900*. Oxford: Clarendon, 1919.

Byatt, A.S. 'Scenes from a Provincial Life.' *The Guardian*, 27 July 2002. http://www.theguardian.com/books/2002/jul/27/classics.asbyatt (accessed 26 May 2016).

Campbell, Joseph. *The Hero with a Thousand Faces*. Novato California: New World Library, 2008.

Capote, Truman. 'The Story Behind a Nonfiction Novel.' Interview with George Plimpton. *The New York Times*, 16 January 1966.

Carroll, Lewis. *Alice's Adventures in Wonderland*. London: Dover Publications; Reprint edition. 20 May 1993.

Carver, Raymond. 'A Storyteller's Shoptalk,' *The New York Times*, 15 February 1981.

Cixous, Hélène, Keith Cohen and Paula Cohen. 'The Laugh of the Medusa.' *Signs* 1, no. 4 (Summer 1976): 875–93.

Coetzee, J. M. *Boyhood: Scenes from Provincial Life*. London: Secker and Warburg, 1997.

Coetzee, J. M. *Elizabeth Costello*. London, United Kingdom: Penguin Books, 2003.

Coetzee, J. M. 'The Novel Today.' *Upstream* 6, no. 1 (Summer 1988).

Conlon, Michael. "Writer Cormac McCarthy Confides in Oprah Winfrey." *Reuters Entertainment*, 5 June 2007. http://www.reuters.com/article/2007/06/05/us-mccarthy-idUSN0526436120070605 (accessed 26 May 2016).

Currie, Mark. *About Time: Narrative, Fiction and the Philosophy of Time*. Edinburgh University Press, 2007.

Damsteegt, Theo. 'The Present Tense and Internal Focalization of Awareness.' In *Poetics Today* 26, no. 1 (Spring 2005): 39–78.

Davidow, Shelley. *The Eye of the Moon*. Portland, OR: The Habit of Rainy Nights Press, 2007.

Davidow, Shelley. *Lights Over Emerald Creek*. Perth: Hague Publishing, 2014.

Davidow, Shelley. 'Qatari Women.' *Sunscripts*: *Florida Suncoast Writer's Conference* (2005).

Davidow, Shelley. *Spirit of the Mountain*. Great Barrington: Steiner Books, 2009.

Davidow, Shelley. *Whisperings in the Blood*. Brisbane: University of Queensland Press, 2016.

De Maupassant, Guy. *Afloat*. Translated by Douglas Parmée. New York: New York Review Books, 2008.
Dickens, Charles. *Oliver Twist*. https://www.gutenberg.org/files/730/730-h/730-h.htm (posted: 10 October 2008, accessed 28 May 2016).
Dillard, Annie. *Living by Fiction*. New York: Harper, 1982.
Doctorow, E. L. 'The Art of Fiction No. 94.' Interview with George Plimpton. *The Paris Review* Winter 101, (1986). http://www.theparisreview.org/interviews/2718/the-art-of-fiction-no-94-e-l-doctorow (accessed 28 May 2016).
Elbow, Peter. *Writing Without Teachers*. New York: Oxford UP, 1972.
Elbow, Peter. *Writing with Power*. New York: Oxford UP, 1980.
Eliot, George. *Essays and Leaves from a Notebook*. Edinburgh: Kessinger Publishing, LLC, 1884.
Eliot, T. S. 'Tradition and the Individual Talent.' In John Hayward (ed.), *Selected Prose*. Middlesex: Penguin Books, 1965.
Fitzgerald, F. Scott. *The Great Gatsby*. New York: Scribner, 2004.
Freytag, Gustave. *Freytag's Technique of the Drama: An Exposition of Dramatic Composition and Art*. Translated by Elias J. MacEwan. Charleston, SC: BiblioBazaar, 2008.
Fuentes, Carlos. *International Herald Tribune*, Paris, 5 November 1991.
Gardner, John. *The Art of Fiction*. New York: Alfred A. Knopf, 1984.
Gass, William H. *Habitations of the Word*, quoted in Frank Kermode, 'Adornment and Fantastication.' *New York Times*, 10 March 1985.
Gass, William H. 'The Soul Inside the Sentence.' *Salmagundi*, no. 56 (Spring 1982): 65–86. http://www.jstor.org/stable/40547536 (accessed 28 May 2016).
Ginsberg, Alan. *Howl and Other Poems*. San Francisco: City Lights Books, 1954.
Greany, Phil. 'An Introduction to Literary Minimalism in the American Short Story,' *what we've got* (blog), 7 February 2012, https://philgreaney.wordpress.com/2012/02/07/an-introduction-to-literary-minimalism-in-the-american-short-story/ (accessed 28 May 2016).
Hassan, Ihab. *The Postmodern Turn*. Columbus: Ohio State University Press, 1987.
Haycock, Lachlan. 'Edge.' Queensland: University of the Sunshine Coast, 2014.
Hemingway, Ernest. *Death in the Afternoon*. New York: Charles Scribner's and Sons, 1932.
Hemingway, Ernest. 'Hills like White Elephants.' In Ann Charters (ed.), *The Story and Its Writer: An Introduction to Short Fiction*, 6th edn. Boston: Bedford/St. Martin's, 2003.

Hemingway, Ernest. *A Moveable Feast*. New York: Charles Scribner's and Sons, 1964.

Hrebeniak, Michael. *Action Writing: Jack Kerouac's Wild Form*. Carbondale: Southern Illinois Press, 2006.

Hugo, Richard. *The Triggering: Lectures and Essays on Poetry and Writing*. New York: W. W. Norton, 2010.

James, Henry. *The Turn of the Screw*. London: Dover, 1991.

James, William. *The Principles of Psychology*. New York, NY: Henry Holt, 1890.

Joyce, James. *Portrait of the Artist as a Young Man*. London: Dover, 1994.

Kelby, N. M. *The Constant Art of Being a Writer: The Life, Art and Business of Fiction*. Cincinnati: Writer's Digest Books, 2009.

King, Martin Luther Jr. 'Letter from Birmingham Jail.' *The Atlantic*, 16 April 2013.

King, Stephen. *Carrie*. New York: Anchor Books, 2011.

King, Stephen. 'Digging up Stories with Stephen King.' Interview with Wallace Strobey. *Writer's Digest*, 16 September 1991. http://wallacestroby.com/writersonwriting_king.html (accessed 28 May 2016).

King, Stephen. 'Why We Crave Horror Movies.' *Playboy*, January 1981.

Koval, Ramona. Interview with Stanley Fish. 'How to Write a Sentence and Read One.' *The Book Show*. ABC Radio National, 24 March 2011. http://www.abc.net.au/radionational/programs/bookshow/how-to-write-a-sentence-and-read-one-stanley-fish/2992106 (accessed 28 May 2016).

Krauth, Nigel. *Creative Writing and the Radical*. Bristol: Multilingual Matters, 2016.

Kristeva, Julia. 'Word, Dialogue, and Novel.' In Toril Moi (ed.), *The Kristeva Reader*, New York: Columbia University Press, 1986.

Lear, Edward. *Nonsense Poems*. London: Dover Publications, 2011.

Lee, Harper. *To Kill a Mockingbird*. New York: Grand Central Publishing, 1988.

LeClair, Thomas. Interview with William Gass. 'The Art of Fiction No. 65.' In *The Paris Review*, no. 70 (Summer 1977).

Le Guin, Ursula. *Steering the Craft*. Portland: The Eighth Mountain Press, 1998.

Lewis, Matthew. *The Monk*. London: Penguin, 2009.

Lodge, David. *After Bakhtin: Essays on Fiction and Criticism*. London: Routledge, 1990.

McCarthy, Cormac. *The Road*. New York: Vintage, 2006.

Moore, Fabienne. *Prose Poems of the French Enlightenment: Delimiting Genre*, New York: Ashgate Publishing, 2009.

Nabokov, Vladimir. *Laughter in the Dark*, New York: Vintage, 1989.
Nabokov, Vladimir. *Strong Opinions*. New York: McGraw-Hill, 1981.
Orwell, George. *Politics and the English Language*. 1946. Reprint. Peterborough: Broadview Press, 2006.
Paul, Annie Murphy. 'Your Brain on Fiction,' *New York Times* 18, 2012.
Pinker, Steven. 'Grammar Puss.' *New Republic*, 30 January 1994. http://www.newrepublic.com/article/77732/grammar-puss-steven-pinker-language-william-safire (accessed 15 November 2015).
Poe, Edgar Allen. *The Tell-Tale Heart*. New York: Bantam Classics, 1983.
Pound, Ezra. 'In a Station of the Metro.' *Poetry,* April, 1913.
Salinger, J. D. *The Catcher in the Rye*. New York: Little, Brown and Company, 1991.
Scholes, Robert E. *Elements of Fiction*. Oxford University Press, 1968.
Skinner, B. F. 'A Behavioural Model of Creation.' In Albert Rothenberg and Carl R. Hausman (eds), *The Creativity Question*. Durham, NC: Duke University Press, 1976.
Smartt Bell, Madison. 'Less is Less: The Dwindling American Short Story.' *Harper's* 272 (April 1986): 64–9.
Spielberg, Steven. 'A Dialogue.' In James M. Cherry, *Rituals of Nostalgia: Old-Fashioned Melodrama at the Millennium. Americana: The Journal of American Popular Culture (1900–present)* 4, no. 2 (Fall 2005). http://www.americanpopularculture.com/journal/articles/fall_2005/cherry.htm (accessed 28 May 2016).
Stewart, Robyn. 'Practice vs Praxis: Constructing Models for Practitioner-Based Research.' *TEXT* 5, no. 2 (October 2001). http://www.griffith.edu.au/school/art/text/ (accessed 28 May 2016).
Temple, Emily. '10 Greatest Charles Dickens Characters.' *The Atlantic*, 7 February 2012. http://www.theatlantic.com/entertainment/archive/2012/02/10-greatest-charles-dickens-characters/252715/ (accessed 28 May 2016).
Traubel, Horace and Gary Schmidgall, eds. *Intimate With Walt: Whitman's Conversations with Horace Traubel*. Iowa City: University of Iowa Press, 1970.
Twain, Mark. *The Adventures of Huckleberry Finn*. New York: Dover Publications, 1994.
Twain, Mark. 'Fenimore Cooper's Literary Offenses.' American Studies at the University of Virginia. http://xroads.virginia.edu/~hyper/HNS/Indians/offense.html (accessed 23 April 2016).
Van Wyk, Chris. 'In Detention.' In Robin Malan, *Poetry Works 1: A Workbook Anthology for Students & Teachers*. Cape Town: David Philip, 1995.

Vonnegut, Kurt. *Slaughterhouse 5*. New York: Dell Publishing, 1969.
Walpole, Horace. *The Castle of Otranto*. London: Joseph Thomas, 1840.
White, Tracey. 'Blackbird.' *Showcase* 5 (January 2014): 44–7. Queensland: University of the Sunshine Coast.
Williams, Paul. 'Cicadas.' *New Contrast 157* 40, no. 1 (2012).
Williams, Paul. *Cokcraco*. Sydney: Lacuna Publishing, 2013.
Williams, Paul. 'Green Island.' *Social Alternatives* 31, no. 2 (2012): 46–51.
Williams, Paul. 'Happy Birthday Frank.' *Perilous Adventures* 11, no. 3 (2007) http://perilousadventures.net/1103/WilliamsFrank.html (accessed 28 May 2016).
Williams, Paul. *Parallax*. Los Angeles: Illusio & Baqer, 2014.
Williams, Paul. 'Promise Me This.' *Chicago Quarterly Review* 14 (2012): 210–16.
Williams, Paul. *Soldier Blue*. Cape Town: New Africa Books, 2008.
Williams, William Carlos. *The Collected Poems of William Carlos Williams, vol. 1, 1909–1939,* edited by A. Walton Litz and Christopher MacGowan, Manchester: Carconet Press, 2000.
Woolf, Virginia. 'Modern Fiction.' In Michael McKeon (ed.), *Theory of the Novel: A Historical Approach*. Baltimore: The Johns Hopkins Press, 2000.
Woolf, Virginia. *Selected Works of Virginia Woolf*. London: Wordsworth Editions, 2007.

Index

A
Adorno, Theodor 44
allegory 108–12, 113
alliterative verse 38–40
allusion 104, 112–13, 139, 160–1
analogy 88, 91, 105, 108–11, 113, 141
antinomacy 168–9

B
Bail, Murray 148
Barthes, Roland 68
Baudelaire, Charles 10
bowerbirding 161–2
Brautigan, Richard 150
bricolage 161–2
Brooks, Gwendolyn 31, 35

C
caesura 31
Campbell, Joseph 144
Camus, Albert 68
Carroll, Lewis 11, 18
Carver, Raymond 92–3 *see also* minimalism
character 37, 92, 101, 119, 121–38, 141–4, 162, 167
  archetypal 145
  historical 176
  types 83–4
  stock 73
  viewpoint 49–59
cliché 82–7, 111, 114
cliffhanger 154
close third person 53–5
close up shot 117
Coetzee, J.M. 84, 87, 148, 157
Cokcraco 133, 165–6, 167–8
comma splices 21–22
composite novel 166–7
conflict 140, 144, 146, 156
contractions (in dialogue) 127
creative non-fiction 172–3
Cummings, e.e. 18

D
Davidow, Shelley 47, 62, 99, 109, 124, 130
dialogue 76, 91, 92, 95, 102, 123–36, 173
dialogue-driven narrative 123
Dickens, Charles 128, 132
direct exposition 123
dispassion 96–7

E
ecriture feminine 169–71
Elbow, Peter 77–8 *see also* Expressivism
Eliot, George 66
ellipses 27
end-stop 31
enjambment 31
epistolary 58–62
ergodic text 167
establishing shot 117
Eucalyptus see Bail
Expressivism 78
exterior and interior landscape 119

F
figurative language 105–8, 120
flashback 152, 168
Flaubert, Gustave 14–15
foreshadowing 152
fragments, *see* sentences, fragments
freewriting 142
freewriting exercises 1, 19, 36, 48, 72, 88, 104, 121, 138, 158
Freytag's pyramid 144

G
Gardner, John 119
Gass, William 32, 36
Ginsberg, Allan 27, 35
grammar 19–36, 78
  minimalist 94
  bad (in dialogue) 127

H
Hemingway, Ernest 90–2
hero's journey 144–5 *see also* Campbell
historiographic metafiction 174–5
Howl see Ginsberg
Hugo, Richard 142–3
hyperbole 113
hypotaxis 95

I
iambic pentameter 42
imagery 105–8 *see also* figurative language
intertextuality 160
intrusive narrator 62
intuitive plotting 141
irony 16, 50, 63–4, 96, 128
  postmodern irony 160
in medias res 151–2

J
James, Henry 24–5, 35, 65
juxtaposition 94, 135, 160

K
Kerouac, Jack 30, 35
'kill your darlings' 99–100
King, Martin Luther 34, 35
King, Stephen 24, 58, 71, 141–2

L
lazy writing 81–2, 85–7
Lear, Edward 12 *see also* limerick
Le Guin, Ursula 2
le mot juste 3, 15 *see also* Flaubert
limerick 12–13
litotes 96

M
magic realism 171–2
maximalism 102–3
McCarthy, Cormac 35, 143
medium shot 117
melodrama 73–5
metafiction 62–3, 71
  historiographic 174
metaphor 82, 99, 104–9, 114, 115, 139, 154, 160
  setting as metaphor 119
metonymy 112–3
minimalism 72, 90–2, 101
  critics of 102
misspellings (in dialogue) 127
multitasking 162–4, 167–8

N
Nabokov, Vladimir 153–4
naming (characters) 131–2
narrator 35, 42, 49–70
  absent 91, 102
  first person 50–1, 52, 54–6, 65–6, 70
  objective 52–3, 96
  omniscient 57–8
  second person 55–6
  third person 52–3
  unreliable 52, 57, 70, 134

O

Orwell, George 82
overwriting 78–80

P

palimpsest 160–1
paragraph 6, 20, 22, 32–5, 40, 41, 46
Parallax 133–4
parataxis 94–5
past tense 67, 69–70
persona 42, 50, 62, 122, 128, 163
Pinker, Steven 19–20, 35
plagiarism 161
plot 136, 138–57
poetry 6, 8–19, 27, 31, 33, 41, 142–3
point of view 48–67, 176
polyphonic voice 162–4
popular writing 85
postmodernism 159–60
practice–led research 141
present tense 67–70

R

repetition 16, 40–2, 45, 48
rhyme 12, 43
rhythm 3, 5, 6, 7, 12, 20, 21, 23, 28, 32, 35, 36–47, 95

S

Scholes, Robert 175–6
sentences 6, 7, 19–35, 44, 45, 65, 79, 95, 100
  construction of 22
  first 146–7
  fragments 21, 27
  lazy 82
  run on 22, 26
sentimentality 73–73 *see also* melodrama
senses, (using the) 113–14, 128, 171
setting 14, 104, 115–120
Shakespeare, William 10–11
simile 82, 83, 107–110, 112, 114
Soldier Blue 29, 34, 35, 63, 75–6, 134, 149, 152–3, 174–5
speech tags (in dialogue) 124–6

spontaneous prose 30 *see also* Kerouac
Steering the Craft see Le Guin
stream of consciousness 65–6
symbol 105, 110–11, 128, 139, 140, 161
synecdoche 112–13

T

The Eye of the Moon 46
theme 53, 89, 90, 131, 143, 155–8, 166–8
Twain, Mark 3

V

verisimilitude 110, 126–7
villanelle 42–3
voice 2, 36–47, 74, 75
  ironic voice 62
  narrative voice 48–62, 163, 166
  polyphonic voice 162
Van Wyk, Christopher 16, 18

W

Whisperings in the Blood 108, 123
white space 26, 33, 98–99, 167
Williams, Paul 13, 29, 34, 35, 53, 56, 63, 76, 97, 118, 132, 133, 134, 149, 152, 153, 163, 174, 175
Williams, William Carlos 7, 13, 18
writing
  bad writing 76–7
  good writing 2, 15, 24, 76, 77, 88, 150
  lazy writing 81–2, 85–7
  overwriting
  popular writing 85
  spontaneous writing 30 *see also* Kerouac, 78 *see also* Whitman
  writing poetry 7
  writing the body 169–70
Writing Degree Zero 68–9 *see also* Barthes
word-association 4–5
word order 16
Woolf, Virginia 19, 65